COMMUNITY DECISION MAKING FOR SOCIAL WELFARE

COMMUNITY DECISION MAKING FOR SOCIAL WELFARE
Federalism, City Government, and the Poor

Robert S. Magill, Ph.D.

University of Wisconsin-Milwaukee

HUMAN SCIENCES PRESS
72 Fifth Avenue   3 Henrietta Street
NEW YORK, NY 10011 ● LONDON, WC2E 8LU

HV
95
. M26

Library of Congress Catalog Number 79-301

ISBN: 0-87705-378-2
ISBN: 0-87705-398-7 pbk.

Copyright © 1979 by Human Sciences Press
72 Fifth Avenue, New York, New York 10011

Printed in the United States of America
9 987654321

Library of Congress Cataloging in Publication Data

Magill, Robert S
    Community decision making for social welfare.

    Bibliography: p. 205
    Includes index.
    1. Social service—United States.   2. Social
service—United States—Finance.   3. Social service—
United States—Citizen participation.   I. Title.
HV95.M26   3611973   79-301
ISBN 0-87705-378-2   ISBN: 0-87705-398-7 pbk.

To Peggy, Andrew, Joanna, and Milton

ACKNOWLEDGMENTS

Community Power and Decision Making: Recent Research and Its Policy Implications, R. S. Magill and T. N. Clark. Reprinted from *The Social Service Review,* Vol. 49, No. 1, March 1975. © 1975 by The University of Chicago.

Federalism, Grants-in-Aid, and Social Welfare Policy, R. S. Magill. Reprinted from *Social Casework,* December 1976. Copyright © by Family Service Association of America, New York.

Who Decides Revenue Sharing Allocations?, R. S. Magill. Reprinted from *Social Work Journal of the National Association of Social Workers,* Vol. 22, No. 4, July, 1977.

CONTENTS

LIST OF TABLES

PREFACE

Community Decision Making for Social Welfare developed over
4 years. It began as a paper for a class in community decision
making taught by Terry N. Clark at the University of Chicago.
It later became a joint article with Professor Clark for a journal.
Further study and research significantly expanded the article
into a Ph.D. thesis at the University of Chicago. Finally, the
thesis was revised substantially for publication as a book.

Writing a book has many solitary moments. One also real-
izes how much others have contributed. At the University of
Chicago, Terry N. Clark gave me his data and encouraged and
helped me. Professors Donnell Pappenfort, Irving Spergel, and
Frank Breul all helped me with the original work that was the
basis for this book. At the University of Wisconsin-Milwaukee,
Walter Trattner reviewed the final draft of Part I and made
many important and useful suggestions. Mary Prawdzik provided substantial help with the computer programming.

The book would not have been possible without the encouragement, support, and assistance of my wife, Peggy. She

always made time for me to work, made many helpful suggestions, and edited the final draft. Finally, I am grateful for the
understanding of Andrew and Joanna who, for a long time,
lived with "Daddy's book."

There are many others who contributed to my thinking
and to the book. I am grateful to them all. I, however, bear full
responsibility for the final product.

Milwaukee   Robert S. Magill

April 23, 1978

A HISTORICAL ANALYSIS OF DIFFERENT APPROACHES TO FEDERALISM AND SOCIAL WELFARE POLICY

Chapter 1

INTRODUCTION

Overview

The relationship of the federal government to the localities in the area of social welfare is the central focus of this book. During Colonial times, local government played a major and significant role by helping those in need of social welfare services. As the country grew, the states and the federal government assumed increasing responsibility for social welfare programs. Today, over half of the federal budget is spent for human services. In recent years there has been a reaction against the size and power of the federal government and a trend toward more community control and decision making.

The first part of the book is a philosophical and historical analysis of the various ways in which the federal government has related to the states and the localities. During the early years of the country's development, the federal government and the states had more separate and equal powers than today. The relationship between the federal government and the states during this time can be called Early Federalism. The role of the national government was more limited under Early Federalism than it is today. All powers not explicitly designated as Federal powers in the U.S. Constitution were assumed to be state powers. Under Early Federalism, social welfare services were provided mainly by the localities and the states.

As the nation grew in size and in complexity, and as its communities became more interdependent, there was a recognition of the existence of broad social problems and the need for a larger federal role. Cooperative Federalism predominated during and after the Great Depression. Cooperative Federalism involved the intermingling of federal and state functions. There was more cooperation between the federal and state governments. Cooperative Federalism promoted, with the Social Security Act, the broad involvement of the federal government in social welfare policy. The conditional grant-in-aid system, in which federal monies are provided to the states and localities for specific purposes and under specific conditions, was greatly expanded under Cooperative Federalism. One consequence of the approach of Cooperative Federalism was the increasing centralization of power in Washington.

The Creative Federalism of John F. Kennedy and Lyndon Johnson was an expansion of the national government into new functions. Creative Federalism also formally recognized the cities as an important unit under federalism. Under Creative Federalism, the central government made grants directly to the cities with little control by the states. Creative Federalism also was a beginning stage in the decentralization of power. Federal monies were provided to the states and localities in the form of block grants. Under block grants, the states and localities are free to choose programs to implement federally established goals. The Community Action Program of the Poverty Program and the Model Cities Program are two examples of block grants under Creative Federalism. Finally, Creative Federalism emphasized the participation of recipients in program decision making.

The pressure for more local control continued. It found its purest expression in General Revenue Sharing, which developed during Richard Nixon's presidency. General Revenue Sharing was characteristic of the New Federalism and was similar, in many aspects, to Early Federalism. General Revenue Sharing returns federal money to states and localities to use for a virtually unrestricted range of purposes. There is almost no federal control. Programs created under the New Federalism emphasize municipal decision making.

Those concerned with the poor and their communities did not welcome General Revenue Sharing. After all, the federal government had created and supported programs that states and localities were unwilling or unable to develop. Advocates for the poor feared that a return to local control would be against the best interests of the poor.

The second part of the book is a study of local decision making for social welfare programs under Cooperative Federalism, Creative Federalism, and New Federalism. Because of the assumption that the trend toward community decision making will persist, the empirical section identifies the factors that can help to explain variations in the size of grants for social welfare programs on the municipal level. The social welfare programs to be considered are the Economic Opportunity Act of 1964, (Poverty Program), the Community Action Section of the Poverty Program, the Demonstration and Metropolitan Development Act of 1966 (Model Cities), and allocations for social services under the State and Local Fiscal Assistance Act of 1972 (General Revenue Sharing). These programs were chosen for the analysis because they all have or can have social welfare goals, they rely, for their initiation, on decision making at the municipal level, and they involve different degrees of federal control.

THE HUMANITARIANS AND THE INDIVIDUALISTS: A PHILOSOPHICAL DISTINCTION

The appropriate role of the federal and local government in social welfare policy can be studied from a philosophical, historical, and empirical perspective. This section will outline briefly and generally the major philosophical distinctions. Later sections approach this question historically and empirically.

The degree and nature of governmental participation in domestic policy is one of the major issues that separates those who traditionally have emphasized individual rights and responsibilities and those who have been concerned with society's responsibilities for people with mental, physical, and social disabilities. Humanitarians emphasize society's responsibilities, while individualists emphasize individual rights and responsibilities. Traditionally, humanitarians have looked to government in general, and the federal government in particular, as an appropriate vehicle for domestic policy. Individualists have resisted all but minimal interference from government. They have felt that democracy and our economy, as well as the individual, could be best served by the absence of governmental involvement and control.

When government is needed, individualists generally have favored the delivery of public services by the lowest level of government. Preference is given to municipal government over state government and states rights before federal involvement. Individualists emphasize the freedom and responsibility of the individual. They fear that too much reliance on government to solve individual problems can weaken freedom and the market form of economy. They feel that both the individual and the society are best served by the relative absence of outside intervention in individual and group problems. Individualists minimize the importance of psychological and sociological forces in the explanation of human behavior.

On the other hand, humanitarians place greater emphasis on biological inheritance and the importance of family, community, and ethnic and class groups in explaining behavior. More so than the individualists, humanitarians explain social problems as the result of a complex interaction of biological, psychological, and sociological forces. Individualists place responsibility for behavior totally on the individual, regardless of background. Humanitarians indict aspects of the society as well as the individual when looking for the causes of social problems, and they look to changes in the society for solutions. Humanitarians naturally have looked to government as an appropriate vehicle for the solution of problems that have developed in the private sector. Individualists have looked to the individual for the solutions to these problems.

From one perspective, the history of the relationship of the federal government to the states and localities is the history of conflicts between those who opposed governmental involvement in various aspects of domestic policy and those who saw government involvement (especially by the federal government) as appropriate when the market and the political system were unable to meet the needs of groups such as children, the elderly, the poor, the mentally ill, and the physically handicapped.

Further, there are differences in orientation between individualists and humanitarians in relation to their view of the way in which the economy should function and the proper way to create public policy in a democracy.

Humanitarians have emphasized that in a capitalist economy, the totally free operation of the market, without outside regulation, inevitably produces social and economic inequality. They assert that the very nature of the market is to distribute resources unequally. The market is based on private gain and competition. Without government interference, society develops large social and economic differences between the rich and the poor.

The modern market system developed after the breakup of feudalism. Even at that time, the private sector and then local government made efforts to supplement the wages of low-income individuals and to provide some relief for the so-called deserving poor. The most famous of these efforts was called Speenhamland. Under Speenhamland, local government supplemented the wages of low-paid employees. Speenhamland was a modified form of what we now call a guaranteed annual income. Recently, individualists such as Senator Barry Goldwater, President Richard Nixon, and Milton Friedman, an economist generally opposed to government interference in the economy, have supported various forms of a Guaranteed Annual Income.

There is now some agreement between humanitarians and individualists that there should be some governmental involvement in social welfare policy. Extreme conflict occurs, however, about questions of how much government participation there should be, the basis on which benefits should be distributed, the levels of the benefits, the degree to which the public and the private sector should participate and the appropriate level of government for the distribution of social welfare benefits.

In terms of the political structure, Americans usually have preferred a form of pluralism, which is analogous to the market. Decisions about who gets what are made in the public arena, often through the competition of interest groups. In a complicated and pluralistic society with many interest groups, policy decisions evolve out of the democratic participation of influential individuals and groups. Individualists feel that these decisions are best made at the governmental level closest to the people. In general, they feel that municipalities and states are more appropriate because they allow for more participation and control by interest groups and the general population than does the federal government.

On the other hand, under a pluralistic philosophy, humanitarians point out that at the municipal level, there are some groups with important needs that do not generally participate in the policy development process. Generally, the consumer of social welfare services, such as children, the unemployed, those addicted to drugs, and the mentally ill, have a difficult time making their voices heard at the municipal level. Major help has been given to these and other needy groups because of the efforts of the federal government.

Furthermore, when decisions are made on the basis of powerful interest groups, there is a tendency for the interest groups themselves to benefit instead of those whom they are supposed to represent. Large institutions, such as business, labor, and powerful social welfare agencies, often are accused of placing their own survival and growth needs before those of their clients. The pluralistic model of decision making benefits the interest groups that are powerful and that participate in the decision making process. The pluralist approach to decision making leaves out large groups of unorganized citizens who normally do not participate in the political process and who are most in need for services.

Some humanitarians feel that social welfare decisions should be made on the basis of expert knowledge and not on the basis of powerful interest groups. Alternative approaches and their costs and benefits and consequences should be analyzed rationally. In an ideal situation, these decisions should be made based on the consideration of the best interests of clients. Under the pluralistic politics model, however, policy decisions are often made on the basis of interest groups, with the most powerful group or groups able to control the goals and means in a particular policy area. Critics of the social welfare system frequently blame the pluralistic and interest group nature of the decision making process for the disorganized, inefficient, and sometimes ineffectual delivery of services.

However, a more rational approach to decision making has the consequence of centralizing decision making. A large program, such as Social Security, cannot be run effectively if each branch office in each state develops its own policies. Long-range planning must be done by experts who are able to determine future needs and problems. However, the centralization of decision making lessens the power and, some assert, the freedom of the individual and makes the growth of big government more likely. Individualists fear this trend as a danger to democracy. Table 1–1 summarizes the difference between the individualistic and humanitarian orientations.

As Table 1–1 indicates, individualists blame social problems on the individual, while humanitarians look to society for

Table 1-1   Differences Between the Individualistic and
Humanitarian Orientations in Social Welfare

	Individualistic	Humanitarian
Cause of social welfare problems	Individual	Society
Primary responsibility for social welfare programs	Individual self-help and private sector	Public sector
Degree of government participation in the economy and in policy	Low	High
Preferred level of government control in social welfare	Lowest (local, state)	Highest (federal)
Method of decision making in social welfare policy	Pluralism (interest groups decide)	Rational (experts decide)

the causes. Individualists feel that the individual and the private sector should have primary responsibility for the solution of social problems. Humanitarians believe that government should solve social problems. Both humanitarians and individualists, while generally committed to a privately controlled, market type economy, agree that there is some role for government to help those who are unable to compete successfully and are in great need. There is disagreement as to the extent to which government should become involved; individualists favor minimal government involvement, and humanitarians support a more active government. Individualists generally favor lower levels of the government, such as the municipalities and the states, as appropriate for the delivery of many domestic services. In the area of social welfare, humanitarians generally favor a greater degree of federal involvement. Finally, individualists support decision making based on the participation of all interest groups without outside controls or preconditions on the nature of the decisions. Humanitarians feel that the pluralistic form of decision making has excluded many very needy persons whose interests have not been considered always by the established interest groups. Humanitarians favor a more rational process, based on the best interests of those not represented in the decision-making process.

After Colonial America, an individualistic orientation generally prevailed. In social welfare, there was a reliance on the market with some help from local and state government and private charity. Policy was developed by powerful interest groups. During the first part of the twentieth century, a more humanitarian orientation became acceptable. There was a recognition that society contributed to the social problems of individuals and that the federal government had an appropriate role in social welfare policy. Presently, the approach of the humanitarians is under attack, and there are strong pressures to return to the individualistic philosophy. The historical sections describe these developments in more detail.

CONCLUSION

Community Decision Making for Social Welfare is based on the assumption that there has been a trend toward more community decision making in all areas of public policy, including allocations for social welfare. It is therefore important for social workers and others to understand the local decision making process and, specifically, to know what community factors are related to allocations for social welfare on the community level.

The book is divided into two major parts. Part I is a historical analysis of different approaches to federalism. Chapter 2 traces the development of Early Federalism and the creation of the conditional grant-in-aid mechanism. Chapter 3 describes Cooperative Federalism and the growing role of the federal government in the creation and delivery of social welfare services. Chapter 4 describes the Creative Federalism of John Kennedy and Lyndon Johnson. To decentralize decision making authority, extensive use was made of the block grant, which allows the states and municipalities to develop means to achieve federally prescribed goals. The Community Action

Program and Model Cities were developed during Creative Federalism. They are block grants and are described in detail in Chapter 4. The New Federalism of Richard Nixon and Gerald Ford is presented in Chapter 5. Special attention is given to a new form of grant, General Revenue Sharing, which furnishes almost total control to states and to localities. Chapter 6 summarizes Part I.

Chapter 7 presents a model of community decision making that has guided the empirical study. The development of community decision making theory, our present knowledge about community decision making, and a description of community variables that are used in the empirical study also are discussed. Chapter 8 describes the sample and research design of the study and the operational measures employed. Chapter 9 analyzes the results of the study. Chapter 10 ends the book with a summary and major conclusions.

The trend toward community decision making impels those concerned with the fate of low-income persons to understand federal-local relationships and the local decision-making process. This area will assume increasing significance in the years to come.

Chapter 2

EARLY FEDERALISM

INTRODUCTION

This chapter and the following three chapters focus on the development, over time, of the relationship among the federal government, the states, and the localities. What different forms has the relationship between the federal government and the state and local governments taken? From a historical perspective, what are the consequences for social welfare policy if the municipal and state governments are most powerful? What are the consequences if the federal government is most powerful?

The way in which our government is organized has been called federalism. Under it, the federal government shares power and responsibility with the states and, more recently, with the cities. This is not the only way to organize government. A more noncentralized approach has been called confederation. Before our Constitution, there was a loose alliance of states. Under the Articles of Confederation, the states had most of the power, and the federal government was relatively weak.

27

On the other hand, there are governments where the central government is very powerful, and other units, such as the states and the cities, derive their power from the central government and are totally dependent on it. These have been called unitary forms of government. Under a unitary form of government, the central government has the power to change or abolish state and local governments.[1]

The approach of American federalism is in between the pattern of control in a confederation of states and those in a unitary state. Under our form of federalism, the states and federal government share power and responsibility in developing and delivering governmental programs. In a broad sense, the various levels of government cooperate with each other.

Table 2-1 presents the form of government and federal and state power.

Table 2-1 Form of Government and Federal and State Power

Unitary	Federalism	Confederation
High federal power	Medium federal power	Low federal power
Low state power	Medium state power	High state power

Under federalism, some functions, such as the defense of the country, are accepted as an appropriate function of the federal government. For other functions, such as fire and police protection in a neighborhood, local governments take responsibility. Then there is a whole group of functions (e.g., provisions for social welfare) that began as local functions, became state and local functions, and is now provided by all three levels of government. The central questions are, under a system of federalism, should the cities, the states, or the federal government provide most social services, or is a cooperative relationship among all three levels of government most desirable?

Just as different countries have different approaches to government (whether it is the unitary approach, federalism, or confederation) so, over time, can there be different emphases within an approach. This pattern of changing emphases has been true of American federalism. Many scholars feel that during the early history of the United States, the federal government had relatively few powers and functions, and the states were considered equal to the central government. It was generally agreed that the powers of the federal government were fixed and immutable. The states were understood to have all powers not explicitly delineated in the U.S. Constitution as federal powers. Some scholars have identified this early period as Dual Federalism. Jane Clark[2] has used the analogy of two rivers, separate but parallel, to describe the relationship between the national government and the states. Other scholars, such as Morton Grodzins[3] and Daniel Elazar,[4] feel that even at this early period, there was a cooperative relationship between the states and the federal government.

During the early nineteenth century there were problems that required national solutions. To solve these problems, the federal government made grants to the states (and to individuals and institutions), first in the form of land and then in the form of money. The states, and later the localities, had the power to administer these programs. To insure control, the federal government eventually placed various conditions on these grants that included the establishment by the federal government of the goals of the programs and the means by which the states would administer the programs. These grants became known as conditional grants-in-aid. They were and are available to state and local governments that choose to apply for them.

During this period of Early Federalism, through the conditional grant-in-aid program and in the courts, there was a continuing effort to determine what functions and how much power were appropriate for the federal government and what were the rights of the states. During this time the scope of all government was much smaller than it is today. Furthermore, there were many areas, such as the provision of social welfare, that were primarily state and local functions.

The Civil War confirmed that, under our form of government, there were certain powers that were not state powers. Although the United States did not become a unitary form of government, America also would not become a loose confederation, with the states maintaining most of the power. The Civil War, the two world wars, and the Great Depression all had the consequence of strengthening the national government vis-à-vis the states.

As the country became larger, wealthier, more complicated, more urbanized, and more industrialized, citizens demanded more services from government at all levels. The idea prevalent before the turn of the century that the least government was the best government was replaced by a feeling that serious social problems should be solved and that solutions could not be accomplished solely by private charity or the free working of the market. In other words, government had a role in helping those who were unable to work because of mental, physical, or social disabilities or because of the scarcity of jobs. Conditions during the Great Depression, when one-quarter of the population could not find any work, clearly demonstrated the need for major intervention by government into the private sector.

With the need for more government and an expansion of the functions of government, a new approach to federalism prevailed. It has been called Cooperative Federalism. Cooperative Federalism is characterized by the national and state governments working together in many of the same areas, sharing power and functions. Under Cooperative Federalism, Morton Grodzins sees the American system of government as analogous to a marble cake, in which there are shared activities and services (even though our government is formally structured like a layer cake, with three layers representing the national, state, and local governments). Under this approach to federalism, decisions regarding a specific function are made at all levels of government, and all levels usually work together in implementing a particular policy.

During World War I and World War II attention was focused on foreign affairs and less emphasis was placed on domestic problems. The pressure for new urban policies grew. Many urban problems erupted with the Civil Rights struggles of the 1960s. Government responded, as it had during the Depression, with several new policies. In addition, there was a new approach to federalism. The Creative Federalism of John Kennedy and Lyndon Johnson emphasized direct federal-city relationships that bypassed the states. Since there had been a large proliferation of conditional grants-in-aid, coordination of grants, especially on the community level, was a major characteristic of Creative Federalism. In addition, there was a growing feeling that the federal government had become too powerful, and efforts were undertaken to decentralize power and decision making to the cities and to the people. The Community Action Program and Model Cities programs are typical of Creative Federalism.

To implement Creative Federalism, reliance was placed on what has been called the block grant. The block grant is similar to the conditional grant-in-aid in all but one major respect. Under the block grant, the federal government establishes the broad goals of the policy, and states and localities have the option to apply or not apply for funds. However, in contrast to the conditional grant-in-aid, states and localities under the block grant are free to establish the means, or programs, that will be used to implement federal goals. The block grant is similar to the conditional grant-in-aid, except that the block grant does not have the conditions. The block grant represents an effort to shift some power and responsibility from the federal government to the states and localities.

For many with an individualistic orientation, Creative Federalism and the block grant did not go far enough in decentralizing federal power. When the Republicans finally won the presidency, Richard Nixon developed what he called New Federalism. A key program that was used to implement this philosophy was General Revenue Sharing. Under General Revenue

Sharing, general-purpose governments such as states, counties, and municipalities automatically receive monies collected by the federal government. In contrast to the conditional grant-in-aid and the block grant, states and localities are not required to write a proposal to receive funds. There are virtually no conditions attached to this money. Governments can select the goals and the means, and there is almost no federal supervision on how the money is spent.

Of the three forms of money transfers from the federal government to the states and municipalities, General Revenue Sharing allows the greatest freedom in municipal decision making. The conditional grant-in-aid gives the federal government the most power, and the block grant is somewhere in between.

General Revenue Sharing represents an important trend toward decentralization of governmental decision making. The remainder of this chapter and the following three chapters describe in more detail how this trend has developed.

Early Federalism

For Daniel Elazar,[5] federalism is the central characteristic of the American political system. Elazar and Grodzins believe that a major aspect of federalism is the idea of the federal union as a partnership between the states and the federal government. Power is distributed among several centers that must negotiate cooperative arrangements with one another to achieve common goals. Under this view, there is a strong federal government and strong state governments. Authority and power are shared, constitutionally and practically.[6] In Elazar's words,

> ... the American federal system has been fundamentally a co-operative partnership of federal, state, and local governments since the early days of the Republic. Within a dualistic structural pattern, the government of the United States has developed a broadly institutionalized system of collaboration based on the implicit premise that virtually all functions of government must be shared by virtually all governments. ...[7]

Or, in the words of Chief Justice Salmon P. Chase, just after the Civil War, The United States is ". . . an indestructible Union, composed of indestructible States."[8]

EARLY CONDITIONAL GRANTS-IN-AID

The relative power and function of the three levels of government—federal, state, and local—are constantly in a state of change. Initially, it was felt that the federal government had only those powers that were specifically identified in the Constitution, and all other powers were state powers.

Since the federal government had no formal authority to impose duties on the states, the conditional grant-in-aid system has developed. As V.O. Key writes, "The grant-in-aid has been utilized to induce the states to undertake functions deemed by Congress to be in the national interest."[9]

The grant-in-aid constitutes a modification of the federal system in which the federal government has no specified authority to assign duties to state and local governments. Key goes on to write that the grant-in-aid ". . . is not solely a legalistic means for the assignment of responsibilities; it is followed by a degree of administrative unification of the two levels of the federal system."[10]

A study of federal grants-in-aid by the Committee on Federal Grants-In-Aids of the Council of State Governments defines federal conditional grants-in-aids as ". . . payments made by the national government to state and local governments, subject to certain conditions, for the support of activities administered by the states and their political subdivisions."[11]

During the early period of federalism, governmental action was needed to develop a system of internal communication to connect the different parts of the nation, to establish a national system of finance, and to create an educational system. According to Elazar, the three levels of government moved to provide services in these areas at virtually the same time.[12]

In general, the earliest grants were land grants. Land was

given to the states by the federal government because it was plentiful, while money was in short supply. In addition, strict constitutional constructionists in Congress, who wanted to protect the rights of the states, were opposed to grants of money from the federal government to the states. They felt that money grants would give the federal government more control. The federal government made grants of land to the states, but the states were permitted to sell this land for money.

There was no significant effort to change this policy until the supply of readily salable land was exhausted toward the end of the 1800s. In 1890, the U.S. Bureau of the Census declared that the land frontier had been closed. Daniel Elazar feels that these early land grants were the predecessors of the modern, conditional grant-in-aid.[13]

The first land grant was made in 1785 under the Articles of Confederation. The Land Ordinance of 1785 provided that lot 16, carved out of federal lands (the Northwest Territory) in each township, should be reserved for the maintenance of public schools. This policy was reaffirmed with the Northwest Ordinance of 1787.

As the nation grew, it was characteristic for the federal government to give land grants to newly created states. For example, one section of each township was granted to the citizens of Ohio for schools when Ohio was admitted into the Union in 1802.[14]

Under terms of the Ohio Contract, the federal government also agreed to construct roads between Ohio and the Eastern seaboard states. For its part, Ohio agreed not to tax public land sold within its boundaries for five years. This was the beginning of a trend under which the states agreed to internal improvements suggested by the federal government if they were paid for by the federal government.[15] In 1848, this grant was increased to include two sections in each township. Fourteen states entered the Union under this provision. Arizona, New Mexico, and Utah, because of the low value of their land, received four sections of federal land in each township when they entered the

Union. Additional grants were made for common school purposes. It is estimated that this program distributed around 130 million acres of federal land to the states. This program culminated in the Morrill Act of 1862, which helped states establish colleges.

Federal land was also given to the states for flood control, wagon road construction, and canal subsidies. In all, it has been estimated that approximately 1,016,200,000 acres of federal land was given to the states. These grants contained almost no requirement for federal supervision or control, except that the lands be used for some purpose, such as education or transportation.[16]

Soon after the Revolutionary War, the federal government assumed the debts of the original 13 states. This program kept many states from going bankrupt. Total grants amounted to $18,271,800. The program contributed to placing state finances on a sound basis shortly after the federal government was established. It can be seen as an early and important step toward a strong central government.[17]

The first direct cash appropriation occurred in 1808, when Congress provided $200,000 to assist in the development of the state militia. This period also saw cash grants for railroads and canals that supplemented the very large land grants given to the railroads.[18]

By the 1830s, the federal government had paid off all of its own debts and had excess funds. In contrast, the states had been borrowing to make internal improvements. State debts had increased from about $13 million in 1820 to more than $174 million in 1837. To relieve the embarrassment of a large federal treasury in the face of large state debts, the Surplus Distribution Act was passed in 1836. It provided for the distribution, at the end of the year, of surplus federal revenue to the states, based on state representations in Congress. Although payments were ostensibly loans, and certificates were given to the Secretary of the Federal Treasury, no repayment was ever made or requested.[19]

During this period, *ad hoc* requests were made by the states to the national government for specific grants. These were usually provided, almost routinely. There were few grant requirements. All major bills for federal monies for canals, harbors, and roads were debated in Congress, with some congressmen favoring federal intervention and others in opposition. By the middle of the nineteenth century, Congress often established investigative committees in response to state requests for federal aid.

In 1859, President Buchanan vetoed a bill that would have provided 20,000 acres of land for each senator and representative in each state to establish state colleges. This presidential veto of a grant was only a temporary setback to those who favored more federal intervention.

In general, during the middle of the nineteenth century, the states did not exert significant pressure on the federal government for grants. Many raised money through their own taxes, such as the property tax, the inheritance tax, and special license taxes. Several states used revenue generated under these taxes to create their own grant-in-aid programs for their communities.[20]

In 1862, Congress passed, by a slim margin, the bill that President Buchanan had vetoed three years earlier. This was the Morrill Act. The Morrill Act was the first major grant-in-aid program to be applied uniformly to all states and territories at the same time. It was based on previous grant-in-aid principles developed over 75 years.[21] The Morrill Act was to help states establish land grant colleges. It provided for the support of state colleges from the sale of national public land. States were required to invest the monies they received from the sale in approved securities. States had to provide for the construction of buildings and make annual expenditure reports to Congress.[22]

The Morrill Act was the first federal grant that carefully spelled out the purpose for which funds could be spent, identified conditions for the use of the money, and required the states to submit annual reports to the federal government.[23]

The first annual federal grant was introduced in 1879 to provide educational materials for the blind. Eight years later, an annual money grant to help the states establish agricultural stations was instituted.[24]

The Education of the Blind Act of 1879 was also the first federal grant based on the principal of need. The Education of the Blind Act provided monies to American Printing House for the Blind for books and equipment. Funds were distributed to the states on the basis of the number of blind pupils enrolled in public institutions in each state.

In 1888, Congress passed a law, also based on need, to care for disabled soldiers and sailors in state homes. Twenty-five thousand dollars was appropriated annually to pay state homes at the rate of $100 per inmate every year. This act was amended in 1889 and required the states to match the federal monies as a condition of receiving the grant.[25]

During this early period, grants changed from land provided by the federal government to service and money. Early grants were often made on an *ad hoc* basis. Over time, these grants became more uniform. The early land grants had general requirements, but specific requirements were gradually developed by the federal government for pre-grant planning and performance. In general, during the early part of our history, planning was unsophisticated. Most attention was given to financial arrangements. Relatively little emphasis was given to state administration of the grants.[26]

EARLY SUPREME COURT DECISIONS

The power of the federal government to distribute land and monies was based on the U.S. Constitution. Article IV, Section 3, Paragraph 2 provided that, "The Congress shall have power to dispose of and make all needful Rules and Regulations respecting the Territory or other Property belonging to the United States. . . ."[27] Since this power was so specific, it never was challenged directly.

Under Chief Justice John Marshall, the Supreme Court emphasized the supremacy of the federal government over the states. The court ruled that the federal government had powers that, while not explicitly stated in the Constitution, were implied. This interpretation of the relationship between the federal government and the states is generally operative today.[28]

However, after the Marshall Court, a different interpretation prevailed. This has been called Dual Federalism by the judicial scholar, Edward S. Corwin.[29] Under Dual Federalism, the distribution of powers between the federal and the state governments is seen as fixed and immutable. The states were seen as equal to the federal government, and all powers that were not explicitly identified in the Constitution as federal powers were state powers.[30]

The approach to federalism characteristic of this period was summarized by Chief Supreme Court Justice Taney in *Abelman* vs. *Booth* (1859). "The powers of the Federal Government, and of the State, although both exist and are exercised within the same territorial limits, are yet separate and distinct sovereignties, acting separately and independently of each other, within their spheres."[31]

In *Hammer* vs. *Dagenhart* (1918), the Supreme Court reaffirmed its position on the powers of the states and localities.[32] The court was asked to enjoin the enforcement of an act passed by Congress that was intended to prevent interstate commerce in the products of child labor. Mr. Justice Day, delivering the majority opinion, stated that ". . . the Nation is made up of States to which are entrusted the powers of local government. And to them and to the people the powers not expressly delegated to the National Government are reserved." Furthermore, the Court held that ". . . if Congress can thus regulate matters entrusted to local authority by prohibition of the movement of commodities in interstate commerce, all freedom of commerce will be at an end, and the powers of the States over local matters may be eliminated and thus our system of government practically destroyed."[33]

THE GROWTH OF ADMINISTRATIVE CONTROLS

The administrative controls placed on federal grants developed gradually. Relatively few controls existed during the nineteenth and early twentieth centuries. With the early land grants, Congress stated goals, but did not provide for administrative units to oversee state implementation of the grants. The courts were used when private rights were adversely affected. However, court action was largely ineffectual. For example, an early study of how the states had administered the Morrill Act for 50 years concluded that every state had at one time violated the legislation.[34]

There was a slow increase of federal control. The Hatch Act of 1887, which provided grants to the states for agricultural experimental stations, required states to report their activities on a regular basis to the U.S. Department of Agriculture (USDA) and the U.S. Treasury Department. Under the Morrill Act of 1890, payments were made to the states for resident instruction in land grant colleges. In order for each state and territory to receive its annual appropriation, its program had to be endorsed by the Secretary of the Interior, who had to authorize the Secretary of the Treasury to distribute monies. Furthermore, payments could be withheld pending an appeal to Congress. First used in 1890, the device of the power of fund withdrawal is now an accepted and powerful element of federal grant legislation.

The Hatch Act of 1887 required state reports. However, this approach did not provide sufficient federal control. In 1894, the Secretary of Agriculture obtained from Congress the right to inspect the accounts and conduct of the local agricultural stations established in the legislation.

This precedent inaugurated the federal audit of state expenditures and the inspection of work undertaken, both now regular features of grants-in-aid. However, inspecting work after it was completed had drawbacks. The Adams Act of 1906 contained provisions requiring states to submit plans to the federal government *before* work was undertaken. This precedent was followed in the Weeks Act of 1911 and the Smith-Lever Act of 1914. In 1921, the Federal Highway Act required federal approval before states could act.[35]

Over time, the conditional grant-in-aid program contributed to increasing federal power. Table 2–2 shows the growth of federal control through the Conditional Grant-in-Aid Program.

The growth in federal control associated with the grant-in-aid program began as the disbursement of federal funds and lands to the states with few conditions. Eventually, the federal government was able to establish the goals and means for program implementation, require the submission of detailed proposals before grants were made, require yearly progress reports from the states, and gain the ability to inspect the actual operation of the grant. If a program did not conform to federal expectations, money could be withheld.

EARLY SOCIAL WELFARE ARRANGEMENTS

Early social welfare practices in this country were based on the English Poor Law. Because of the shortage of labor and a generous system of land tenure, there was no widespread poverty. Jobs and land were abundant, and the early colonists were concerned about providing good treatment for the poor.

In his book *From Poor Law to Welfare State: A History of Social Welfare in America*,[36] Walter Trattner writes that provision of help for the poor in Colonial America had the following characteristics:

—it was undertaken by the smallest unit of government,

—long term cases were housed with individual families at public expense,

—short term cases were given outdoor relief,

—help was limited to the residents of a town; outsiders often were refused aid,

Table 2-2   The Increase in Federal Control Through
the Conditional Grant-in-Aid Program

Date	Grant name	Purpose	New aspect of federal control
1785	Land Ordinance of 1785	Provide federal lands	First grant
1808	Militia Grant	Help states establish militia	First cash grant
1862	Morrill Act	Help states establish colleges for working class	Identified conditions for use of money; yearly reports by states
1879	Education of the Blind Act	Educate the blind	First grant distributed on basis of need
1887	Hatch Act	State agricultural stations	Regular state reports to USDA and U.S. Treasury
1890	Morrill Act of 1890	State residents' instruction in land grant colleges	Review and endorsement by Secretary of Interior before state could receive money; payments could be withheld pending state appeal to Congress
1894	Modification of Hatch Act of 1887	Increase powers of Secretary of Agriculture	Secretary of Agriculture could inspect accounts and conduct of local agriculture stations
1906	Adams Act	Agricultural research, experiments	States submit detailed plans before work was undertaken (this precedent was followed in the Weeks Act of 1911 and the Smith-Lever Act of 1914)
1921	Federal Highway Act	Complete interstate highways	Federal approval before states could act (more involved than in the agricultural area)

—poor, illegitimate, and orphaned children were apprenticed out,

—mentally ill persons were treated the same way as were the poor. They were boarded out at public expense. As public institutions began to appear, many mentally ill people were placed in them.

These arrangements were adopted quite early in our history. Trattner reports that in 1642 the Plymouth Colony had developed provisions for the poor. This was followed in 1646 by Virginia, in 1673 by Connecticut, and in 1692 by Massachusetts. During colonial times, Trattner feels that "most communities attacked the problem of poverty with a high degree of civic responsibility."[37] They spent a considerable amount of money and, at least at the country's founding, were more concerned with the condition of the poor than with cost.

However, during the late seventeenth century and early eighteenth century, the number of poor persons grew significantly. This growth resulted from many factors. Increased immigration brought some individuals unable to adjust to the new world. Frequent wars and battles, including those with the French and Indians, added disabled soldiers and refugees from the frontier to those in poverty. Especially along the New England seacoast, fishermen were lost at sea, and their wives and children were left indigent. In addition, since fishing was a seasonal occupation, all those connected with it—fishermen, longshoremen, and craftsmen—were unemployed for part of the year and needed assistance. Illegitimacy rates rose in both the North and the South, and more children had to be cared for at public expense. Further, natural disasters, such as fires and diseases of all types, led to greater numbers of citizens needing aid. Finally, economic depressions caused hardship for many.[38]

Walter Trattner writes that while private charity was limited in scope in the seventeenth century, private giving increased during the eighteenth century. The increase occurred because private fortunes began to grow, and wealth was more widely distributed. In addition, popular religious and secular movements of the time encouraged private charity.

The Revolution caused social and economic dislocations and resulted in the disruption of many community administered poor law measures. Localities often were overwhelmed with indigent persons and increasingly turned to the states for help. In addition, classical economists in Europe were attacking some of the Poor Law approaches. It was felt that providing too much help for the poor would lead to a population of poor citizens too large for society's resources. Further, a large poverty class would constitute a drag on society and retard progress.

In addition, as communities grew larger and more impersonal, it became more difficult to take care of the poor, the handicapped, and the mentally ill by having them live in private homes. There was a trend towards building institutions, or almshouses, to take care of the poor. For example, in 1824, New York State enacted the County Poorhouse Act. This measure provided for the building of one or more poorhouses in each county of the state. Poorhouses were to house all recipients of public assistance. The cost was to be paid by the county out of tax funds. In addition, the act provided for the creation of a new group of welfare officials, County Superintendants of the Poor, to administer the almshouse.

Walter Trattner writes that while there were other types of relief, the almshouse became the most widely used. For example, there were eighty-three almshouses in Massachusetts by 1824. There were 180 almshouses fifteen years later and 219 by 1860.[39] Kathleen Woodroofe writes that the almshouse sheltered the old, the young, the sick, the poor, the emotionally ill, the blind, the addicted, and the criminal. Paupers could be farmed out from the almshouses, and children were still apprenticed to businessmen or farmers. Some avoided the almshouse and received public outdoor relief. However, relief was kept at subsistence levels, and the names of the recipients were placed on a pauper roll that was often reproduced in the newspapers.[41]

In the beginning almshouses were community based, autonomous, and undifferentiated. Eventually, the cost of the services increased, and some cases required institutional care beyond the capacity of local units. State agencies were created for certain groups requiring institutional care. Virginia established a state hospital for the insane in 1773; Kentucky, a home for the deaf in 1823; Ohio, a home for the blind in 1837; and Massachusetts, a home for juvenile delinquents and the retarded in 1848.[41]

An early example of limited federal involvement in social welfare is the Hartford (Connecticut) Asylum founded in 1819 by Thomas Gallaudet for the education of the deaf. Originally, it was a formal cooperative program involving the federal government and the six New England States, with other states participating informally. In 1819, Congress granted one township in Ohio to the institution, which was renamed the American Asylum for the Deaf and Dumb (it is now known as the American School for the Deaf). The township in Ohio was to be either sold or leased with the funds placed in a permanent fund, and the interest was to be used to help pay for the school. This money was matched by grants from the state legislatures. The school was required to make annual reports to the contributing states and to the federal government. Students were accepted from all states in the Union, although particular emphasis was placed on New England.

In addition to the federal land grant, the New England states made annual appropriations for the maintenance of the institution. The school was designed as an experimental institution to encourage the establishment of similar schools by other states. It was also created to encourage federal participation in the education of the handicapped. A second school was founded in Kentucky in 1823 and obtained a federal grant three years later. In 1857, Thomas Gallaudet's son, Edward, was made head of a newly created school for the deaf in the District of Columbia. An outgrowth of this school was Gallaudet College, the first college for the deaf. Federal monies were appropriated during the Civil War for faculty and buildings for Gallaudet College.[42]

The movement to provide education for the deaf with federal involvement owed a lot to the ability of Thomas Gallaudet. Another strong and effective crusader was Dorothea Dix, who established many state mental institutions. For example, the New Hampshire State Insane Asylum, founded in 1842, resulted from Dorothea Dix's early efforts. Funds were provided by the federal government's surplus distribution of 1837. State land, matching the federal funds that were channeled through the town, was provided for the institution.[43]

Before the Civil War, American war veterans were given land grants instead of cash pensions. This practice was similar to the federal government practice of providing states with land that they could sell instead of providing direct cash grants. This procedure was followed because the federal government had a large amount of land, while cash was scarce. When farming was a major occupation, the land grant to individual veterans was a major means of advancement.

The first 13 states originally made grants of Western lands to their soldiers. However, all states did not own Western lands and, even before the signing of the Declaration of Independence, land-poor states began agitating to stop this process. By 1790, all Western lands (except those owned by Georgia), were federally owned. It was traditional for states to provide land in the West to veterans. This provision of land was done with federal involvement and supervision.[44]

In 1854, President Pierce vetoed a bill, inspired by Dorothea Dix, that would have granted the states federal land for the indigent insane. President Pierce argued that if this bill became law, Congress would then be able to provide assistance for all indigent persons and thus transfer what had been a state and local responsibility to the federal government.[45] The President said, ". . . I cannot find any authority in the Constitution for making the Federal Government the greater almoner of public charity throughout the United States."[46]

During the beginning of Early Federalism, the powers of the federal government and the states were separate and more or less equal. Jane Clark has described Early Federalism as follows: ". . . viewed from a distance, the landscape of government in the United States appears to contain two separate federal and state streams flowing in distinct but closely parallel channels."[47]

However, over time there was a gradual and steady increase in federal power. This was reflected in federal conditional grant-in-aid legislation and by the actions of the executive branch of government in the administration of grants. In social welfare, incomplete and uncoordinated efforts by private charities were supplemented by government, first at the local level and then at the state level. Taken as a whole, these efforts were clearly inadequate, and federal help was needed. Resistance to federal intervention in social welfare was dispelled by the crisis created by the Great Depression of 1929. In addition, the Great Depression required that the federal and state governments work more closely together than they had in the past. This new relationship between the federal and state government has been called Cooperative Federalism.

NOTES

1. Claudius O. Johnson, H. Paul Castleberry, Daniel M. Ogden, Jr. and Thor Swanson. *American National Government,* fifth ed. New York: Thomas Y. Crowell, 1960, p. 124.

2. Jane Clark. *The Rise of a New Federalism: Federal-State Cooperation in the United States.* New York: Columbia University Press, 1938, p. 8.

3. Morton Grodzins, ed. by Daniel J. Elazar. *The American System: A New View of Government in the United States.* Chicago: Rand McNally, 1966.

4. Daniel J. Elazar. *American Federalism: A View From the States.* New York: Thomas Y. Crowell, 1966.

5. Ibid., p. 2.

6. Ibid.

7. Ibid., p. 297.

8. *Texas* vs. *White,* 74 U.S. (7 Wall.) 700 (1869).

9. V. O. Key. *The Administration of Federal Grants to the States.* Chicago: Public Administration Service, 1937, p. 4.

10. Ibid., p. 4.

11. Report of the Committee on Federal Grants-In-Aid of the Council of State Governments, *Federal Grants-In-Aid.* Washington, D.C.: The Council of State Governments, 1949, p. 29.

12. Elazar, p. 25.

13. Ibid., p. 143.

14. Grodzins, p. 18.

15. Earl M. Baker, Bernadette A. Stevens, Stephen L. Schechter, and Harlan A. Wright. *Federal Grants, The National Interest and State Response: A Review of Theory and Research.* Philadelphia: Temple University, Center for the Study of Federalism, p. 20.

16. Committee on Federal Grants-in-Aid, pp. 2–4.

17. Ibid., p. 1.

18. Michael D. Reagan. *The New Federalism.* New York: Oxford University Press, 1972, p. 56.

19. Committee on Federal Grants-in-Aid, pp. 1–3.

20. Baker et al., pp. 20–21.

21. Elazar, p. 219.

22. Baker et al., p. 22.

23. Key, pp. 6–7.

24. Ibid.

25. Grodzins, p. 37.

26. Baker et al., p. 24.

27. U.S. Constitution, Article IV, Section 3, Paragraph 2.

28. Reagan, pp. 19–20.

29. Edward S. Corwin. *The Twilight of the Supreme Court.* New Haven, Conn.: Yale University Press, 1934.

30. Ibid.

31. *Ableman* vs. *Booth,* 62 U.S. (21 How.) 506 (1859).

32. *Hammer* vs. *Dagenhart,* 247 U.S. 251 (1918).

33. Ibid.

34. S. P. Capen, in *Proceedings of the Association of American Agricultural Colleges and Experiment Stations,* 1915, pp. 141–142.

35. Key, pp. 27–31.

36. Walter I. Trattner. *From Poor Law to Welfare State: A History of Social Welfare in America.* New York: The Free Press, 1974, pp. 15–27.

37. Ibid., p. 26.

38. Ibid., pp. 29–30.

39. Ibid., pp. 44–62.

40. Kathleen Woodroofe. *From Charity to Social Work in England and the United States.* Toronto: University of Toronto Press, 1962, p. 84.

41. Ibid., p. 85.

42. Walter I. Trattner. "The Federal Government and Social Welfare in Early Nineteenth-century America." *Social Service Review, 50,* June 1976, 243–255.

43. Elazar, pp. 119–120.

44. Ibid.

45. Extract from *Congressional Globe* (Thirty-Third Congress, 1st Session, May 3, 1854), pp. 1061–1063. Reprinted in S.P. Breckinridge, *Public Welfare Administration in the United States: Selected Documents.* Chicago: University of Chicago Press, 1938. Reprinted in Breul and Wade, p. III–D1.

46. Ibid., p. 111–D2.

47. Clark, p. 8.

Chapter 3

COOPERATIVE FEDERALISM

INTRODUCTION

Scholars disagree about when Cooperative Federalism began. Some, like Morton Grodzins, believe that elements of Cooperative Federalism have existed since the beginning of the country and became dominant after 1935.[1] Others identify programs developed in response to the problems created by the Great Depression as totally different from Early Federalism.

Michael Reagan writes that under Cooperative Federalism, ". . . the national and state governments work together in the same areas, sharing functions and therefore power."[2] There is cooperation in running programs. In contrast to earlier periods, the stress is less on the legal and constitutional positions of the levels of governments. Instead, there are "intergovernmental relations" based on practical working relationships. Since there has always been a resistance to federal operation of local programs, there is, for Reagan, a ". . . compromise of shared functions, permitting both national stimulation and financing and state and local operation of programs to take necessary variations in application into account."[3]

Compared to earlier approaches, Cooperative Federalism, in operation, meant an increase of federal power. In a series of decisions, the Supreme Court overthrew the idea that the federal government was confined to the powers specifically mentioned in the Constitution, with all other powers reverting to the states. During Cooperative Federalism, Supreme Court decisions upheld the philosophy of Alexander Hamilton and the court decisions of Chief Justice Marshall that the U.S. Constitution implied powers that were the domain of the federal government, and the states could not prohibit the federal government from functioning in these areas. The practical effect of these interpretations was that the states were no longer treated as coequal partners, as they had been under Early Federalism. The federal government had virtually unlimited powers.

In the area of social welfare, until 1935, the federal government did not provide broad social welfare programs. Consequently, most welfare efforts were undertaken by state or local government or by private charities. However, the passage of the Social Security Bill in 1935 and the confirmation by the Supreme Court of its constitutionality provided a precedent for federal support of social welfare that completely changed the way in which American society cares for those in need.

On an ideological level, politicians and the general public began to accept a greatly increased role for the federal government. An approach to social problems that recognized the influence of the environment on individuals and groups replaced the individualist orientation (expressed through Social Darwinism), of the middle and late nineteenth century. The philosophy of elevation of the individual, the survival of the fittest, and a limited role for government lost favor and support. In its place came the feeling that the federal government had a responsibility to intervene in the economy and in social welfare programs of the private sector and of lower levels of government. Nowhere was this trend more evident than in the growing and congested cities. At the turn of the century, the country was changing from a rural, agrarian society to an urban, industrialized society. People were moving to and living in the cities. They came from rural areas and, in large numbers, from foreign countries. Eventually, the cities took their place alongside the states as an important part of the federal system.

The federal income tax law, passed in 1913, began a very dramatic shift of resources away from the cities and the states and toward the federal government. The Great Depression, two world wars, and the Korean War furthered the accumulation of power in Washington. What started out at the beginning of the twentieth century as cooperation between the federal and state levels of government became, by the middle of the century, a less equal relationship. The federal government had the resources and the power to use them. State government was, by and large, unwilling or unable to deal with the predominantly urban problems that were emerging. There was a proliferation of federal conditional grant-in-aid programs. Near the middle of the twentieth century, the federal government had grown so fast and so large that there was a growing recognition that more noncentralized policies would have to be pursued. At the end of Cooperative Federalism, a trend for the devolution of power from the federal government to the states and localities was emerging.

EARLY SOCIAL WELFARE PROGRAMS

A new approach to the role and responsibility of government in relation to the economy and to those in need began around 1900. According to Richard Hofstadter, "the relatively untrammeled capitalism of the nineteenth century was beginning to change into the welfare capitalism of the twentieth; the frustrations of the middle class and the needs of the poor were accelerating the change. Men sensed that a different order was slowly arising."[4]

For Hofstadter, previous reform and protest movements had been disjointed and uncoordinated uprisings of workers and farmers. At the beginning of the twentieth century, middle-class citizens started to fear the large private business and financial enterprises that were being created by individuals such as Henry Ford, Andrew Carnegie, John D. Rockefeller and Andrew W. Mellon. Middle-class Americans worried that their status and standard of living could disappear. "In a society of great collective aggregates, the traditional emphasis upon the exploits of the individual lost much of its appeal."[5] The progressive movement captured the attention and support of the fearful middle class.

With its campaign for a wide range of reforms, the Progressive movement laid the groundwork for later expansions of governmental authority. As Robert Bremner writes:

> Nearly all of these reforms involved limitations on private property rights and extension of public authority into areas previously regarded as the exclusive preserve of individual initiative. Taken one by one, the proposals were neither novel nor drastic. Collectively, however, they implied that a new attitude toward politics and economics was taking shape. . . . They demonstrated a strong tendency to substitute public benefit for private profit as the measure of industrial efficiency. At the time of its formulation supporters of the program called it "preventative social work." Today, when most of it has been adopted, we recognize it as the core of "the welfare state."[6]

It is difficult to imagine the social welfare system without the active participation of the federal government. However, the precedent established by President Pierce, in vetoing the bill that would have granted federal lands for the poor mentally ill in 1854, generally guided federal relief policy for almost three-quarters of a century. Pierce felt that the U.S. Constitution did not authorize federal involvement in social welfare. This ruling was used to discourage major federal programs for those in need. However, before the passage of the Social Security Bill in

1935, the federal government had developed some relatively small welfare-related efforts.

For example, the Bureau of Refugees, Freedmen, and Abandoned Lands (Freedmen's Bureau) was created within the War Department in 1865 and continued until June 1872. The Freedmen's Bureau developed numerous programs for the hungry. It created schools and asylums for the young and the illiterate, employment services for freedmen, and courts and legal aid for helping newly freed slaves to learn their rights as citizens. During its existence, the Bureau distributed $17 million in goods, services, and cash. It operated 45 hospitals, transported 32,000 freedmen and white refugees, and helped provide 4,000 teachers for Southern schools.[7]

In 1912, after a long controversy, the Children's Bureau was established within the Department of Labor to investigate and report on all matters relating to the welfare of children. The Children's Bureau was charged with investigations regarding infant mortalities, birthrates, children's institutions, juvenile courts, desertion, dangerous occupations, accidents and diseases, employment, and legislation affecting children. Julia Lathrop, a social worker, a former resident of Hull House, and a founder of the United Charities of Chicago, was the first chief. She was succeeded in 1921 by another social worker from Chicago, Grace Abbott.[8]

In 1918 the Infancy and Maternity or Sheppard-Towner Bill was introduced into Congress. The bill provided federal aid to the states to help them improve their maternal and child health facilities and services. Special attention was given to rural areas where such programs were especially lacking or inadequate. The government was to provide conditional grants-in-aid, on a matching basis, to states that agreed to establish facilities and services such as public health nursing and education, outpatient clinics, hospitals, and improved inspection of maternity homes in accordance with guidelines established by the Children's Bureau. State health departments were to administer the grants.[9]

After three years of bitter conflict, the Sheppard-Towner bill became law. It authorized an annual appropriation of $1,-252,000 for a five-year period, later extended to seven years. Through the Sheppard-Towner Act, almost 3,000 child and maternal health centers were established in 45 states, primarily in rural areas. The Sheppard-Towner Act strengthened state health departments and helped to encourage the development of county units. Furthermore, the Sheppard-Towner Act brought the federal government into the field of child welfare through the area of health. Walter Trattner writes, "On the foundation laid by the Infancy and Maternity Act—the first statute to provide federal grants-in-aid to the states for a welfare program other than education—were reared many of the cooperative federal-state programs established under the Social Security Act of 1935."[10]

In 1922 a legal case that challenged the constitutionality of a federal conditional grant-in-aid reached the Supreme Court. Early in 1922 the Attorney General of Massachusetts concluded that the Sheppard-Towner Act was unconstitutional. In *Massachusetts* vs. *Mellon,*[11] the state argued that the Sheppard-Towner Act was unconstitutional because (1) it assumed powers not granted to Congress, (2) it provided for an unconstitutional delegation of federal powers to the states, (3) the appropriations were not for national purposes but for local purposes, (4) federal grants-in-aid imposed on the states an unconstitutional choice between yielding to the federal government a part of their rights and powers reserved by the Tenth Amendment or losing a share of appropriations that they would otherwise be entitled to under the grant statutes, and (5) the grant funds were not distributed proportional to the tax effort of each state.[12]

On June 4, 1923, the Supreme Court dismissed the case on the grounds that it had insufficient jurisdiction, thus upholding the constitutionality of the grant-in-aid as exemplified by the Sheppard-Towner Act. The court held that "We have no power *per se* to review an annual act of Congress on the ground that they are unconstitutional."[13] The power of the court is in determining that an act is applicable to a controversy. In effect, the court ruled that grants-in-aid will not be declared unconstitutional and that the court does not have jurisdiction to determine the merits of the constitutional questions involved in grants-in-aid.[14] In other words, in *Massachusetts* vs. *Mellon,* the Supreme Court established the constitutionality of conditional grants-in-aid.

In 1920 Congress passed the controversial Vocational Rehabilitation Act. It provided $1 million a year for the states to aid disabled veterans, with the federal government matching the state share on a 50–50 basis. The Vocational Rehabilitation Act of 1920 was met with strong resistance from state and local public health officials who felt it was a federal infringement on their authority.[15]

The public health functions of the states have been aided by several federal laws. The National Board of Health was created in 1879. Although short-lived, it was an important precedent.

Beginning in 1917, Congress provided small sums annually for studies of rural sanitation and demonstration projects. These funds allowed cooperation with state and local governments in the operation of health departments in rural counties. By 1930, demonstration projects in rural health were being conducted in 204 counties in 24 states. This appropriation was discontinued with the passage of the Social Security Act which authorized grants to states for the extension of general public health programs.

The Chamberlain-Kahn Act of 1918 was primarily a war measure and provided funds to assist states in the prevention and control of venereal diseases. Within a few years, appropriations were discontinued under the Chamberlain-Kahn Act. However, the Sheppard-Towner Act continued to provide aid to the states to promote infant and maternal health.[16]

FEDERAL SOCIAL WELFARE PROGRAMS DURING THE GREAT DEPRESSION

According to Gaston Rimlinger, the Depression of the 1930s found America unprepared to deal with the problems of economic insecurity typical of a modern, industrial society. While workmen's compensation was widespread, it was generally inadequate.[17] All but four states had workmen's compensation laws by 1930. However, in 12 of these states, coverage applied only to hazardous occupations. In many of the other states, the worker bore 50 to 80 percent of the cost.[18]

Many states had been providing some form of public assistance before passage of the Social Security Act of 1935. The first law on a state level that provided aid for dependent children was passed in 1911. The first old age assistance law was passed in 1914. By 1934, 27 states had some form of old age assistance, 45 states had some form of state aid to dependent children, and 27 states had some form of aid to the needy blind. Many of these state laws consisted primarily of enabling legislation to permit local jurisdictions to fund and administer these services. In 1934, there were approximately 180,000 recipients of some form of old age assistance. Approximately 280,000 dependent children were receiving aid.

The growing economic depression placed increasing pressures on local and state welfare systems. The crisis drastically changed people's attitudes about federal government. As Gaston Rimlinger writes, "The expectation now was that the government somehow had to take charge of the economy; it had to become responsible for the general performance of the system."[19] The local and state welfare systems and the private insurance companies had been unable to meet a clear, pressing, and national need. Specific federal intervention was all that was left.

The federal government first became involved in the area of emergency relief in 1932 with the establishment of the Reconstruction Finance Corporation (RFC). The RFC was authorized to make loans of up to $300 million to states and localities to relieve destitution. Later the law was changed to read that the loans did not have to be repaid. The RFC became a grant-in-aid type program.

The Federal Emergency Relief Administration (FERA) was established in 1933. It represented the largest short-run program in the history of grants-in-aid. Between 1933 and 1936, FERA made grants-in-aid to the states of $3 billion; approximately two-thirds of this was spent in 1935. The grants were used for work relief and direct relief, although the federal government favored the former. Direct relief was made in cash or in kind to those who were unemployed. FERA was different from previous grant-in-aid programs in that federal administrators were given almost complete discretion in the allocation of federal aid. Ultimately, they had the power to take over and administer a state program if it was not being operated properly.

The Civil Works Administration (CWA) operated concurrently with FERA. In about three months during 1933 to 1934, it spent almost $1 billion. Through the CWA, state Public Welfare Agencies became agencies of the federal government, and the federal government paid workers who were on CWA projects directly.

The Works Progress Administration, later called the Works Projects Administration (WPA), was established in 1935 to replace FERA. The WPA developed and administered a new work relief program for all unemployed workers. It was a federal program. The national government determined the policy and administered the program, with some state and local government participation. During its existence, WPA spent over $10 billion in federal funds, the largest amount spent so far for any single relief program. In addition, the administrator of WPA was given "more extensive authority with respect to the distribution of public funds and the control of local activities than any other governmental officer in time of peace."[20]

Finally, the Federal Emergency Administration of Public

Works was established in 1933. Later known as the Public Works Administration (PWA), it created public works programs. PWA provided both grants and loans. ". . . The Public Works Administration broke with all earlier grants-in-aid precedents by establishing direct federal-local relationships with reference to the states."[21]

On August 14, 1935, the Social Security Act was approved and became law. It has been called, ". . . one of the major events in the history of federal grants-in-aid."[22] The original bill provided for a nationally administered old age insurance system, which we now know as social security. Compulsory contributions from employees and employers in covered occupations financed the insurance system. Under the Social Security Act states also were encouraged to establish and administer unemployment compensation programs, and federal monies were available to operate these programs under the public assistance provision.

The original social security bill provided federal grants-in-aid to states for the needy aged and blind and for families with dependent children. More recently, aid to the blind, the elderly poor, and the disabled has become part of the nationally administered social security system. The state and/or county administered public assistance programs serve families with dependent children. Public assistance funding comes from both federal and state monies.

Among other provisions, the Social Security Act required states to make programs available in all political subdivisions and established federal minimum standards for eligibility. Within broad limits, the states were free to establish the scope of their public assistance programs. "The enactment by Congress in 1935 of a broad social security program, based on the grant-in-aid devise, resulted in an increase in 1937 to the highest level of regular grant expenditures yet reached, and also laid the groundwork for future increases."[23] In 1936, the federal government paid over $28 million for the public assistance program. Over $24 million was for old age assistance. In 10 years the total federal outlay was over $421 million, of which approximately $352 million was for old age assistance, $58 million for aid to dependent children, and the rest for aid to the blind.[24]

COURT DECISIONS RESULTING IN INCREASED FEDERAL POWER

"In spite of its shortcomings . . . the Social Security Act reversed the policy pursued for a century and a half by the federal government of leaving the care of the indigent to the states."[25] A series of Supreme Court rulings paved the way for the expansion of the federal government into providing for the general welfare and also defined a broader role for the federal government in relation to the states.

For example, the argument in *United States* vs. *Butler*[26] revolved around the true meaning of the phrase, "to provide for the general welfare of the United States" in the Constitution. James Madison had asserted that the welfare phrase in the Constitution was merely a reference to other powers enumerated in subsequent clauses of that section. Madison's interpretation was that federal power was limited. Federal power included the ability to tax and spend for the general welfare. Spending for the general welfare was limited to the enumerated legislative areas committed to Congress. Madison had an individualistic orientation.

On the other hand, Alexander Hamilton argued that the phrase "to provide for the general welfare" conferred to Congress broad powers that could be derived from this phrase. In this view, Congress has the power to tax and to legislate in order to provide for welfare activities not specifically identified in the Constitution. In the *United States* vs. *Butler* the Supreme Court, in effect, ruled that although certain provisions of the Agricultural Adjustment Act of 1933 were in conflict with the Constitution, the U.S. Congress did have the right to grant federal monies for specific purposes to "provide for the general welfare."[27] This was an important ruling, since it established the constitutional basis for federal intervention in social welfare.

The next year, the Supreme Court ruled on the validity of the Social Security tax on employers of eight or more persons. In *Steward Machine Company* vs. *Davis*[28] Justice Cardozo, writing on behalf of the Supreme Court, declared that the tax imposed by the Social Security Act on employers was valid and the federal government's right to establish old age insurance was constitutional.[29]

In *United States* vs. *Darby*,[30] the Supreme Court was asked to rule on whether Congress has the power to prohibit interstate commerce where employees do not receive the minimum wage and whether Congress can prohibit the employment of workers at other than prescribed wages and hours in the production of goods for interstate commerce. The court reversed an earlier position (*Hammer* vs. *Dagenhart*, 1918) and ruled that Congress has the power to govern interstate commerce and that this power extends to the regulation of intrastate commerce, which has a substantial effect on interstate commerce. The court went further and stated that:

> Our conclusion is unaffected by the Tenth Amendment which provides: "the powers not delegated to the United States by the Constitution, nor prohibited by it to the States are reserved to the States respectively, or to the people." The amendment states but a truism that all is retained which has not been surrendered. There is nothing in the history of its adoption to suggest that it was more than declaratory of the relationship between the national and state governments . . . or that its purpose was other than to allay fears that the new national government might seek to exercise powers not granted, and that the states might not be able to exercise fully their reserved powers. . . .[31]

In effect, *United States* vs. *Darby* eliminated earlier legal restrictions on federal power.[32] In other words, Congress had the right to expand its powers and functions unilaterally from those originally enumerated in the Constitution. This was a return to the judicial doctrine of Chief Justice John Marshall. In this decision, the Supreme Court permitted Congress to do things not specifically mentioned in the Constitution. There is thus no permanent division of authority between the federal government and the state governments.[33]

INCREASE IN THE AMOUNT SPENT FOR CONDITIONAL GRANTS-IN-AID

As Figures 3–1 and 3–2 indicate, there has been a dramatic growth in federal reliance on the conditional grant-in-aid. Although its form was established during the period of Early Federalism, it was not until Cooperative Federalism that the conditional grant-in-aid mechanism was employed to any large degree. In 1902, for example, federal expenditures for all grants-in-aid were slightly over $3 million. By 1932, government efforts to stimulate the economy resulted in a federal expenditure for conditional grants-in-aid of $162 million. After the Great Depression, programs were canceled and there was a dramatic cutting back in expenditures under the conditional grant-in-aid approach. The low point was reached in 1934, when only $26 million was spent. Since that time, as Figure 3–1 shows, expenditures using the conditional grant-in-aid form have increased dramatically. In 1936, the federal government spent $100 million in grants-in-aid and in 1939 over $500 million by 1947, the figure rose over the $1 billion mark.[34] During the early and middle 1950s, the federal government was spending between $2 and $3 billion a year under the conditional grant-in-aid. This figure doubled in the late 1950s and early 1960s. For example, in 1960, over $6.5 billion was being spent by the federal government on conditional grant-in-aid programs.[35] Figure 3–2 shows federal expenditures for state and local government from 1960 to 1978. It includes all federal

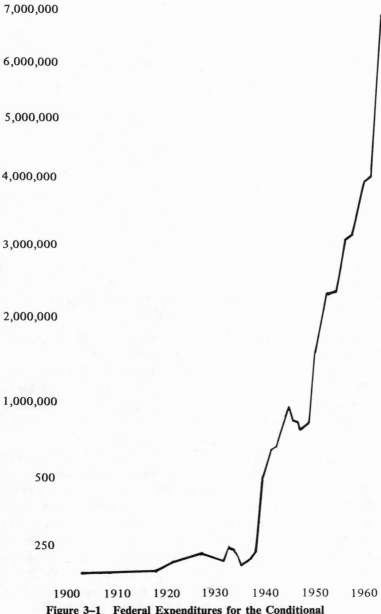

**Figure 3–1   Federal Expenditures for the Conditional
Grant-In-Aid Program**

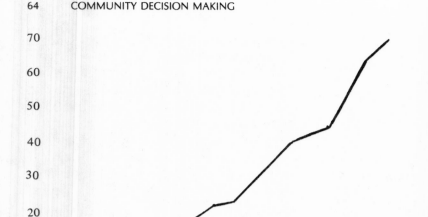

Figure 3–2   Federal Expenditures for State and Local Governments

expenditures to state and local government, such as spending for all types of grants, loans, and shared revenues.

Figures 3–1 and 3–2 show that from 1945, there has been a constant increase in the amount of federal money available to states and localities. During the 1960s, there was also an expansion of the types of state and local functions that were supported by federal monies. Grants-in-aid were provided by the federal government for school lunches, airports, hospitals, civil defense, elementary, secondary, and higher education, the economic development of depressed areas, health for the poor, urban renewal, and relief from poverty. By 1967 there were 85 separate program categories; 17 were established between 1931 and 1945, 29 between 1946 and 1960, and 39 from 1966 to 1967.[36] The Advisory Commission on Intergovernmental Relations estimated that in 1970, there were 530 conditional grant-in-aid programs. Of these, four-fifths were passed after 1960, and 143 were instituted during the first two years of Richard Nixon's presidency.[37]

COOPERATIVE FEDERALISM   65

ADMINISTRATIVE PROCEDURES RESULTING IN INCREASED FEDERAL POWER

It has been shown that there was a dramatic increase, during the first half of the twentieth century, in the dollar amounts that the federal government distributed to the states and localities through the conditional grant-in-aid program. There was also an increase in the types of functions that involved federal resources and federal expertise. The decision by the Supreme Court that the federal government could provide for the general welfare and that the states could not prohibit federal participation in functions not listed as federal powers in the Constitution established the legal basis for this federal expansion into functions that had previously been seen as the province of the states and localities or the private sector. The establishment of the federal income tax in 1913 provided the federal government with the resources to increase government expenditures generally, including expenditures under the conditional grant-in-aid mechanism.

Under the conditional grant-in-aid, as it evolved, the federal government establishes the goals and means for programs, which are administered by the states and localities. States and localities have the freedom to apply or not to apply for specific grants.

Martha Derthick, in her book, *The Influence of Federal Grants: Public Assistance in Massachusetts*,[38] writes that the accumulation of federal power through the grant-in-aid mechanism has been accomplished in several ways. The selection of subjects for the public agenda is the first step in determining the public policy process. By offering grants, the federal government is able to force consideration of a program on the state and local level. The existence of a federal grant provides the opportunity for state and local actors who agree with the national policy to pressure local or state government to apply for the federal conditional grant-in-aid. Federal sponsorship reduces the risk to local administrators of making a proposal and taking

subsequent action. Both monetary and political risks, if problems arise, can be transferred to the federal government.[38] In
other words, state and local administrators can blame problems
on the federal government. Furthermore, the availability of
federal programs increases the cost of state and local inaction.
By not applying for grants, localities are losing federal money
and become vulnerable to the charge of failing to take advantage of federal funds.

Federal influence also affects the content of the proposal.
During informal discussions between applicants and federal
administrators, federal direction can be ensured.

Federal grant-in-aid programs often have created a new
agency at the state or local level. Although the local agency
might start out apart from its federal counterpart, in the long
term it inevitably becomes a federal ally. The independence is
lost because the local agency is dependent on its national counterpart for funds. In effect, the local agency becomes the local
representative and the communications channel of the federal
government.

Once a grant is received, the federal oversight function
tends to concentrate on proper administration, on the process
of policy instead of its substance. According to Derthick, the
concentration on process occurs because administrators on the
federal, state, and local levels are more aware of and interested
in administration. Also, dealing with administrative matters is
less controversial than dealing with policy conflicts. However,
by creating appropriate administrative structures, federal administrators can determine policy directions.

The ultimate federal power lies in completely withholding
money, but withholding funds rarely is used because it serves
no one's interests. Objections come from Congress. Relations
between federal administrators and the states and localities are
damaged. And, once funds are withheld, the federal government is unable to continue to influence state and local agencies.
It is more common for federal administrators to threaten the
withholding of a grant or to withhold part of the funds.[39]

While there is the potential for federal involvement in state and local policies and operations under the conditional grant-in-aid program, there is not total federal control. The programs are administered by the states and the localities. In general, national agencies do not make day-to-day decisions. They do not exercise continual direction or supervision.

The grant-in-aid program creates the conditions for cooperation and collaboration between the various levels of government. According to Morton Grodzins, the grant-in-aid programs have ". . . transferred more funds between national and state governments, involved more civil servants, framed more far-reaching policies, and led to greater administrative interaction than any other single factor in the national-state operation."[40]

From Early Federalism, where for the most part, all powers not explicitly provided to the federal government were reserved to the states, through Cooperative Federalism, where the federal government, along with the states, had the power to provide for the general welfare, there had been a dramatic increase in federal power vis-à-vis the states and localities. While this trend was to continue, at the same time, beginning pressures toward decentralization and local coordination culminated in a new pattern of federal-state relationships—Creative Federalism. In the dramatic growth of federal power were the seeds of decentralization. The next chapter describes the beginning of this shift.

NOTES

1. Morton Grodzins; ed. by Daniel J. Elazar. *The American System: A New View of Government in the United States.* Chicago: Rand McNally, 1966, pp. 51–57.

2. Michael D. Reagan. *The New Federalism.* New York: Oxford University Press, 1972, pp. 20–21.

3. Ibid., pp. 22–23.

4. Richard Hofstadter. *Social Darwinsim in American Thought.* Boston: Beacon Press, 1955, p. 119.

5. Ibid., p. 119.

6. Robert Bremner. *From the Depths: The Discovery of Poverty in the United States.* New York: New York University Press, 1960, p. 138.

7. Victoria Olds. "The Freedmen's Bureau: A Nineteenth-Century Federal Welfare Agency." *Social Casework,* **44,** May 1963, 251–252.

8. Blanche D. Coll. *Perspectives in Public Welfare: A History.* Washington, D.C.: U.S. Government Printing Office, U.S. Department of Health, Education and Welfare, Social and Rehabilitation Service, Office of Research, Demonstrations and Training, Intramural Division, 1969, pp. 73–74.

9. Walter Trattner. *From Poor Law to Welfare State: A History of Social Welfare in America.* New York: Free Press, 1974, pp. 185–186.

10. Ibid., p. 187.

11. *Massachusetts* vs. *Mellon,* 262 U.S. 447 (1923).

12. Report of the committee on federal grant-in-aid of the council of state governments, *Federal Grants-In-Aid.* Washington, D.C.: The council of state governments, 1949, p. 21.

12. Committee on Federal Grants-In-Aid, p. 21.

13. *Massachusetts* vs. *Mellon.*

14. Committee on Federal Grants-In-Aid, Ibid.

15. Earl M. Baker, Bernadette A. Stevens, Stephen L. Schechter, and Harlan A. Wright. *Federal Grants, The National Interest and State Response: A Review of Theory and Research.* Philadelphia: Temple University, Center for the Study of Federalism, p. 28.

16. V. O. Key. *The Administration of Federal Grants to the States.* Chicago: Public Administration Service, 1937, pp. 15–16.

17. Gaston Remlinger. *Welfare Policy and Industrialization in Europe, America and Russia.* New York: John Wiley, 1971, p. 199.

18. Bureau of Labor Statistics, *Handbook of Labor Statistics,* 1931, published as Bulletin No. 541. Washington, D.C.: U.S. Government Printing Office, 1931, p. 479.

19. Rimlinger, p. 199.

20. Committee on Federal Grants-In-Aid, p. 175.

21. Ibid., pp. 175–176.

22. Ibid., p. 148.

23. Ibid., p. 34.

24. Ibid., p. 152.

25. Kathleen Woodroofe. *From Charity to Social Work in England and the United States.* Toronto: University of Toronto Press, 1962, p. 174.

26. *United States* vs. *Butler,* 297 U.S. 1 (1936).

27. Ibid.

28. *Steward Machine Company* vs. *Davis,* 301 U.S. 548 (1937).

29. Ibid.

30. *United States* vs. *Darby,* 312 U.S. 100 (1941).

31. Ibid.

32. See Chapter 2.

33. Reagan, Ibid.

34. Committee on Federal Grants-In-Aid, p. 32.

35. Grodzins, p. 61.

36. Anita S. Harbert. *Federal Grants-In-Aid: Maximizing Benefits to the States.* New York: Praeger, 1976.

37. Reagan, pp. 55–56.

38. Martha Derthick. *The Influence of Federal Grants: Public Assistance in Massachusetts.* Cambridge, Mass.: Harvard University Press, 1970.

39. Ibid., pp. 196–219.

40. Grodzins, p. 60.

Chapter 4

CREATIVE FEDERALISM

INTRODUCTION

The 1960s were a period of ferment and change. Domestic problems had received relatively little federal attention during the presidency of Dwight Eisenhower. A series of factors came together during the first part of the 1960s that resulted in the most significant advances in social welfare policy since the Great Depression. On a structural level, a new approach to the relationship between the federal government, the states, and the cities was developed. It has been called Creative Federalism.

Deteriorating conditions in the cities were among the nation's major domestic problems. The cities had long been a neglected part of the federal system. Cities are creatures of the states and are legally dependent on states. The Iowa Supreme Court ruled in 1863 that "municipal corporations owe their origin to, and derive their powers and rights wholly from, the legislature. . . . It may destroy, it may abridge and control municipalities. . . ."[1] This decision is known as Dillion's rule, after the Iowa Supreme Court justice who wrote it. Dillion's rule defined the legal status of cities. Under it, cities are dependent on the states. However, given the strong tradition of local self-rule, states have granted cities the right of home rule, or the right to govern their own affairs.

Since 1920, the urban population had exceeded the rural population, and federal payments to the cities had been increasing since 1932.[2] However, the major relationship in the federal system had been between the national governments and the states. In the early 1960s, recognizing the problems of the cities, ". . . Congress for the first time authorized aid to local communities for a virtually unrestricted range of functions. . . ."[3]

During the 1950s there was a sluggish economic growth, a rise in unemployment, a serious problem of racial inequality, and problems related to automation and migration to the cities. For example, in 1953, unemployment was 20 percent higher among blacks than among whites. Between 1953 and 1963, the average differentials rose to 112 percent.

From the middle of the twentieth century, there had been a migration of poor blacks from the South to Northern, Midwestern, and Western cities. Between 1950 and 1960, 1,400,000 blacks left the South. This movement resulted partly from the mechanization of Southern agriculture. The influx placed serious pressure on the economies and public welfare systems of these cities.[4] Little attention was paid to these problems by the administration of Dwight Eisenhower.

In the 1960s, the country was in the midst of the Civil Rights Movement. It was becoming increasingly clear that the social and economic integration of minority persons into American society could be accomplished only by federal action. The Civil Rights Movement exerted strong pressure on all levels of society to respond to the needs of minorities. One consequence of the Civil Rights Movement was a growth in voting participation by minorities. Some feel that President Kennedy owed his slim victory over Richard Nixon in the 1960 presidential election to the voting of minorities, especially blacks, and that the Poverty Program was created as a repayment for this vote.

The approach toward government was also different in the 1960s; John Kennedy and Lyndon Johnson were elected as activist presidents. After the relative quiet of the 1950s, the country was ready for the federal government to deal directly with urgent domestic problems. In addition, the country was in a period of prosperity. There was a federal budget surplus which could be used for new domestic programs.

In the 1950s the country's problem solving was complicated by the conflict existing between a Republican president and a Democratically controlled Congress. Major domestic legislation was stalemated. In the 1950s the Democrats in Congress and in the Democratic Advisory Council, a policy group established outside of Congress, developed policies that although not enacted, became the party platform of the 1960 presidential election. This program included environmental protection, jobs for the unemployed, federal aid to education, medical care for the elderly, a civil rights program, and a program for the poor. When the Democrats won control of the presidency and the Congress, many of these proposals developed in the 1950s were enacted into law.[5]

Outside of Congress, there were experiments by the private sector that eventually would be translated into national legislation. Outstanding among these experiments were the so-called Grey Area Projects sponsored by the Ford Foundation. The Grey Area Projects took a community-based approach to the problems of juvenile delinquency. Through a combination of planning and community action, various Grey Area Projects attempted to mobilize community agencies to help delinquent youth. In conjunction with the President's Committee on Juvenile Delinquency, the approach of the Grey Areas Projects was destined to be the model for the Community Action Program of the War on Poverty Program.[6]

Although close, the election of President Kennedy signaled that the country was ready for an activist stance on domestic matters. Kennedy headed a party that had a reasonably unified domestic program, developed during the long Eisenhower years.

However, the mood of the country was not reflected in the archaic committee structure of Congress, which was dominated by conservative Southerners who were reelected year after year. The conservative House Ways and Means Committee was crucial to any congressional action, since it could stop legislation from reaching the floor of the House. According to James Sundquist, President Kennedy decided on a strategy of enlarging the membership of this committee in order to make it more liberal. In a crucial vote on the House floor, the administration won by five votes. President Kennedy realized that his total legislative program hinged on a five-vote margin.[7]

After President Kennedy was assassinated, President Lyndon Johnson started his term with a significant amount of public sympathy and support. Johnson's election victory over Barry Goldwater was overwhelming. Johnson's landslide also helped to bring many Democratic congressmen into office. In 1964, the country had an activist Democratic Congress and an activist Democratic president. More important, the composition of significant congressional committees, such as the House Ways and Means Committee, was changed enough to make legislative action possible. A truly historic Congress passed more domestic legislation than any other Congress since the New Deal. Many of the proposals developed between 1953 and 1960 became law. Among other things, Johnson told Congress, "This Administration today, here and now, declares unconditional war on poverty in America."[8]

CREATIVE FEDERALISM

During the early 1960s, there was increased questioning of Cooperative Federalism. The dramatic proliferation of grants developed during Cooperative Federalism was creating confusion, and inefficiency was a major concern in Washington. A significant element of the new approach was an effort to consolidate and coordinate programs and administrative structures.[9]

This approach has been called Creative Federalism.[10] To a greater extent than before, direct federal-city relationships that bypassed the states were emphasized. In addition, Creative Federalism initiated contractual relationships between federal agencies and nongovernmental organizations.[11] Finally, decentralization provided local officials with more discretion in determining objectives and means to implement federally prescribed goals.

To accomplish these changes, greater reliance was placed on the block grant. The block grant resembles the conditional grant-in-aid in two of its features. Under both the block grant and the conditional grant-in-aid, states and localities take the initiative in applying for funds. The federal government establishes the policy goals under both the conditional grant-in-aid and the block grant. The block grant differs from the conditional grant-in-aid because it gives states and localities the freedom to select the means (i.e., the specific programs) to implement the federally developed goals. In contrast to the conditional grant-in-aid, the block grant is a step in providing states and localities with more decision making authority.

An early example of Creative Federalism is found in a study dealing with public housing. Gilbert Steiner reports that the study recommended in December 1960 that federal subsidies for housing should be made available to local governments for use in a locally determined fashion. The study urged that the federal statute be drawn broadly in order to accommodate a wide variety of local governmental conditions. Steiner writes that the ". . . proposal was really a proposal for what Lyndon Johnson would later call Creative Federalism."[12]

According to James Sundquist and David Davis, federal concern for better management and coordination was reflected in a number of administrative actions. The Vice-President was made a liaison with state and local governments. The Bureau of the Budget created a staff to concentrate on consolidating grant-in-aid programs. Integrating mechanisms were developed at the community level. By 1967, there were more than a dozen types of federally initiated, local, coordinating structures. The Departments of Agriculture, Labor, Commerce, and Health, Education and Welfare each had at least one community-based coordinating body. Each was different and reflected at the local level the constituencies of the parent federal agency.[13] The Model Cities program is an excellent example of this approach to coordination. As Derthick writes, "Through the Model Cities program, the federal government was offering localities a reward if they themselves could contrive a way of coordinating federal activities."[14]

Decentralization of power and decision making also was a part of Creative Federalism. John Gardner, later to become Secretary of the Department of Health, Education and Welfare, was fearful that the federal government was overpowering the states and localities. He wrote that "We must revitalize the state and local leadership so that it can play its role vis-á-vis an increasingly powerful federal government; we must revitalize . . . so they can play a vital role in the partnerships without being completely submerged and obliterated."[15] One way to achieve this objective was to restrict the development of specific grants-in-aid. Local leadership and competence would develop if they were not always dependent on the federal government.[16]

Decentralization began to be stressed in a different way; it was understood as the dispersion of power to the people. As Richard Goodwin, a close advisor to President Kennedy, wrote, the goal ". . . must be to meet specific ills through methods which can in themselves enlarge the sense and reality of individual relevance and participation. . . . Both burden and enterprise must be shifted into units of action small enough to widen the outlets for direct participation and control."[17]

The Development of the Community Action Program of the Poverty Program

The Poverty Program consisted primarily of conditional grant-in-aid programs designed to help the poor, and especially poor youth. One of the most innovative sections of the Poverty Program was the Community Action Program. The Community Action Program was a block grant to eligible communities. It was based on experimental programs which were developed during the early 1960s.

The most famous of these early programs were sponsored by the Ford Foundation and the President's Committee on Juvenile Delinquency. The President's Committee on Juvenile Delinquency grew out of John Kennedy's concern for youth. Its purpose was to create a new federal initiative against delinquency.

According to Peter Marris and Martin Rein, the Grey Area Projects developed from problems created by urban renewal and the lack of responsiveness of inner-city schools. This approach was broadened to a more general attack on the social and economic conditions that produced the ghetto. The Grey Area Projects were based on the assumption that poverty was multicaused, that it resulted from inadequate social and economic institutions. Eventually, Ford Foundation sponsored programs were initiated in selected urban areas such as Boston, Oakland, New Haven, Philadelphia, Washington, New York City and, on a state level, in North Carolina.[18]

The President's Committee on Juvenile Delinquency had a limited budget—$6 to $8 million annually. It therefore confined itself to making grants for the planning of community programs and supplemented Ford Foundation programs. The financing of the specific programs that grew out of the general plans were left to local agencies or to grant-in-aid programs from state and federal sources. By the end of 1963, community programs in more than a dozen cities had been funded.[19]

The theoretical rationale for this approach was provided

by Richard Cloward and by Lloyd Ohlin, an advisor to the President's Committee in *Delinquency and Opportunity.*[20] Cloward and Ohlin felt that all Americans, rich or poor, shared certain culturally prescribed goals. These included the attainment of wealth, power, and status.

However, the legitimate means to attain these commonly held goals were distributed differentially throughout the social structure. Access to the institutions that could help an individual to achieve these culturally prescribed goals, such as education and jobs, was less available to lower-class youths. Lower-class youths, aware of the limited opportunity to achieve their aspirations, engaged in delinquent behavior more often than middle-class youth.

The way in which a youth dealt with blocked aspirations depended on his or her subculture. In a neighborhood where there was an organized criminal subculture, adults served as role models. A criminal subculture developed around stealing, which was regarded as an apprenticeship to recruitment into the world of the professional criminal. In a disorganized neighborhood, where adult role models were not integrated, a conflict subculture developed. This type of neighborhood was characterized by fighting gangs and violence. Youths growing up in either of these two types of neighborhoods used what Ohlin and Cloward identified as illegitimate opportunity structures to achieve culturally presented goals.

Finally, there were individuals who adopted neither approach because of specific behavior patterns or because they failed at delinquency. Their predominant response was to retreat through the use of drugs. Therefore, if one was going to solve the problem of delinquency, the major effort should be aimed at changing the social structure and providing a legitimate opportunity structure for youth.[21] This theory was the basis of Mobilization for Youth, an experimental delinquency control project on the Lower East Side of New York City that was funded by both the Ford Foundation and the President's Committee on Juvenile Delinquency.[22]

According to Peter Marris and Martin Rein, these new, community-based, social action agencies, formed to combat juvenile delinquency, embodied many of the dilemmas facing American social reformers.[23] For example, the approaches of planning, politics, and democratic participation were often in conflict. The needs of democratic participation or political expedience frequently were not similar to the elaborate, rational approaches developed by the planners.

The local community agencies were dependent on federal monies, foundation grants, and the cooperation of local institutions such as the public schools. Because of this, the local agencies were unlikely to attempt basic reforms of the sponsoring agency. Community agencies were reluctant to attack agencies that sponsored them and provided them with financial support. According to Marris and Rein, these early community action approaches ended in liberal reform. The local community agencies were unable to make basic changes. Instead, their projects attempted to stimulate innovation and responsiveness in the agencies that they attempted to change.

There were also structural problems faced by the sponsors. Marris and Rein feel that the Ford Foundation lacked a legitimate base within the political structure from which to organize reform. The federal government's dilemma arose from the many agencies, each with its own interests and constituencies, that tried to influence the final program in separate and often conflicting ways. It was difficult for the President's Committee on Juvenile Delinquency to organize a coordinated, coherent package.

Finally, and perhaps most important, with a problem such as poverty, which is multicaused, and in a pluralistic society, comprised of a variety of competing interest groups, one or two funding sources were unable to develop a rational, integrated master plan. Local community action agencies funded by the President's Committee on Juvenile Delinquency and the Ford Foundation often were placed in the position of judging competing ideas and interests instead of advocating for special approaches.

For Marris and Rein, the process of reform in American society involves the progressive campaigning for incompatible alternatives. What is important is movement—to keep the process going. The constant need is to develop ideas to disturb the equilibrium. The danger is deadlock, when competing views create inaction. The result of this process, according to Marris and Rein, is the steady enlargement of possibilities. Democracy cannot impose solutions, as a despotic society would. It can create activity. The American reformer must somehow make circumstances more favorable for reform without extinguishing all of the energy.

After five years of experience prior to the Poverty Program, Marris and Rein felt that the Grey Area Projects, among others, had not solved intractable problems such as the difficulty of changing institutions, the conflict between participation and planning, the difficulties of opening up opportunities for low-income minority youths, and the conflict between grassroots community action and government sponsorship. However, community action did create a range of skills, concepts, organizations, and models of action. It had stimulated some realignment of resources on the local level. Finally, when the federal government was ready to develop the Poverty Program, policy advisors eagerly adopted the familiar concept of community action.[24]

If nothing else, the work of the Ford Foundation and the President's Committee on Juvenile Delinquency demonstrated a need and an approach to working on ghetto problems. However, Marris and Rein felt that their failures as well as their successes were not adequately considered. Because the new Community Action Program of the Federal Anti-Poverty Bill was modeled after these projects, it was destined to repeat many of the problems contained in the Grey Area Projects.

The Poverty Program was also a response to the growing awareness of the existence of serious poverty in a rich society.

The prevailing economic view in the 1950s was the "trickle down theory," which asserted that as the country prospered, the poor would share in benefits, and the percentage of those in poverty would be diminished. There was some disagreement with this view. According to Sar A. Levitan,[25] John Kenneth Galbraith felt that prosperity would not solve the problem of poverty. In 1950 and again in 1955, Senator John J. Sparkman of Alabama documented the persistence of rural poverty in hearings in front of the Joint Economic Committee. Beginning in 1955, Senator Paul Douglas of Illinois regularly pointed to pockets of poverty in the midst of plenty. In 1959, Robert J. Lampman, a staff member of the Council of Economic Advisors, made a systematic statistical analysis of poverty.[26] He brought this analysis to the attention of top officials in the Kennedy White House and got support from Walter Heller, Chairman of the President's Council of Economic Advisors. Heller eventually took the lead in organizing proposals for the Poverty Program.[27]

Michael Harrington's book, *The Other America* (published in 1962), described the existence of serious poverty in the U.S. It helped to educate the public and prepare the way for a national initiative against poverty.[28]

There were other factors that set the stage for a national commitment to poverty reduction. John Donovan writes that the Task Force on Manpower Conservation, established by President Kennedy in 1963, concluded almost a year later, that one-third of the nation's youth, on examination, was found unfit for military service.[29] Poverty was the main reason that the youths failed either the mental or physical exams. The committee included Labor Secretary Willard Wirtz, Defense Secretary Robert McNamara, HEW Secretary Anthony Celebrezze, and General Lewis B. Hershey. The report was entitled "One Third of a Nation" and was authored by Daniel P. Moynihan, then Assistant Secretary of Labor. Upon releasing the report, President Johnson announced, "I shall shortly present to the Congress a program designed to attack the roots

of poverty in our cities and rural areas . . . This war on poverty
. . . will not be won overnight."[30]

While the society was in turmoil, there was no organized
group of low-income persons pressuring the federal government
for a poverty program. Robert Haverman suggests that because
of this, the program was developed primarily by social scientists
and others in the administrative branch of government.[31] For
example, during the summer and early fall of 1963, a joint
Council of Economic Advisors–Bureau of the Budget Task
Force was created to develop the information for designing an
attack on poverty. Levitan reports that this task force thought
in terms of a limited budget and did not devise specific operational programs. Two days after the assassination of President
Kennedy, Walter Heller met with President Johnson. Johnson
is reported to have said, "That's my kind of program. It will
help the people. I want you to move full speed ahead on it."[32]

Proposals from the administrative departments—Agriculture, Labor, Commerce, Health, Education and Welfare—
started to flow in. There was the problem of the appropriate
administrative structure for the new program. It was agreed
that a new unit would be established in the executive office.
Because coordinating all the agency proposals on the federal
level was difficult and because only limited funding was possible, a new approach was needed. Levitan reports that David L.
Hacket, Executive Director of the President's Committee on
Juvenile Delinquency, believed that the techniques developed
by his committee might be adapted to fighting poverty on a
broader scale. Hacket believed that an effective antipoverty
program would require a coordinated effort that was not feasible under existing single-purpose grant-in-aid programs. The
community action approach of the Grey Area Projects and the
President's Committee on Juvenile Delinquency became the
focus in antipoverty planning.

The proposal had support for a number of reasons. It
appeared to have substantive merit, and it also lent itself to

budgetary flexibility. "The program could be sold as a comprehensive attack upon poverty that allowed experimentation and adaptability to local situations. . . . The approach also provided a new area of experimentation for the coordination of general-purpose federal grants in line with the President's later stresses on 'Creative Federalism.' "[33]

John C. Donovan, in his book, *The Politics of Poverty,* speculates on another advantage of community action. Elections are won because people are registered and get to the polls. In the American electorate, the largest group of apathetic, nonparticipants is the poor. What better way to "politicize" the poor than to get them involved in the neighborhood development activities sponsored by the Community Action Program. As Donovan writes, "President Johnson's declaration of war on poverty may have been a supremely political act on the part of a supremely political man."[34]

Paul Peterson and J. David Greenstone seem to concur with this conclusion. They write that instead of emphasizing service delivery or lessening economic inequality, the Community Action Program became an attack on political poverty. The goal was to increase the political participation of previously excluded citizens, with special emphasis on black Americans. Peterson and Greenstone feel that community action was successful in reducing the political poverty of blacks.[35]

The Poverty Program legislation was drafted in the White House with no congressional involvement. It was rushed through Congress, and probably would have failed if Lyndon Johnson had not made a strong effort for its passage.[36]

According to Levitan, no overall plan guided program selection in the Poverty Program. Instead, programs were distributed to existing federal agencies based on their proposals.[37] The Department of Labor got the Neighborhood Youth Corps. The Department of Health, Education and Welfare got the Work Experience and Training Program, the Adult Basic Education Program, and the Work-Study Program. Rural antipoverty loans were administered through the Department of Agriculture, and financial assistance to small businesses was handled by the Small Business Administration. The Office of Economic Opportunity (OEO) itself ran Volunteers in Service to America (VISTA), the Job Corps Program, and the Community Action Program. According to Daniel Moynihan, the planners ". . . wanted a program that would pass Congress, help win the Presidential election, and eliminate poverty, in perhaps that order."[38]

The programs in the Poverty Program, except the Community Action Program, were primarily conditional grants-in-aid. The Community Action Program was a block grant. Under the Community Action Program, communities established community action agencies composed of civic, business, educational, political and social service leaders and representatives of the poor. The local community action agencies were charged with creating a program to combat poverty. As the program developed, community action agencies would apply to other federal departments for conditional grants-in-aid to fund their program. Federal departments were directed to give highest priority to proposals for grants-in-aid from community action agencies.

According to Levitan, the Bureau of the Budget had an early interest in the block grant approach of the community action concept. They saw community action as a devise for coordinating federal programs on the community level.[39] Further, community action involved a minimum amount of new money, since local community action agencies would apply for existing conditional grants-in-aid. The community action approach had the advantage of creating the image of a broad attack on poverty.[40] The Community Action Program was an early effort at a new approach to transfer monies between the federal government and the cities. As Levitan wrote, "The multi-purpose CAP is an alternative to the traditional special-purpose grant-in-aid, and in this respect approaches the concept of the block grant."[41]

THE COMMUNITY ACTION PROGRAM

The community action approach was included as Part A of
Title II of the Economic Opportunity Act of 1964.[42] The Economic Opportunity Act contained seven titles. Title I provided
for youth programs such as the Job Corps, the Neighborhood
Youth Corps, and the Work-Study Programs. Title II, in addition to providing for the Community Action Program, created
Adult Basic Education Programs. Title III included programs
to combat rural poverty, including the provision of loans and
programs for migrant workers. Title IV provided for help for
small businesses, and Title V provided for work experience
programs through public assistance.[43]

The Community Action Program was publicized as a new
approach to combating poverty and a good example of Creative
Federalism. In the Economic Opportunity Act of 1964, Section
201 (a) of Part A, Title II, defining a community action program, read as follows.

A. The term "community action program" means a program
1. which mobilizes and utilizes resources, public or private, or
   any urban or rural, or combined urban and rural, geographical area (referred to in this part as a "community"), including but not limited to a state, metropolitan area, county, city,
   town, multicity unit, or multicounty unit in an attack on
   poverty;
2. which provides services, assistance, and other activities of
   sufficient scope and size to give promise of progress toward
   elimination of poverty or a cause of or causes of poverty
   through developing employment opportunities, improving
   human performance, motivation, and productivity, or better-
   ing the conditions under which people live, learn, and
   work;
3. which is developed, conducted, and administered with the
   maximum feasible participation of residents of the areas and
   members of the groups served; and
4. which is conducted, administered or coordinated by a public
   or private nonprofit agency (other than a political party), or
   a combination thereof.[44]

At the end of the first year, fiscal 1965, 415 local communities had organized themselves and had applied for and received grants to organize community action agencies. These grants totaled $237 million. There were 48 Job Corp Centers, 59 Vista projects, 639 Neighborhood Youth Corp projects, Adult Basic Education Projects in 40 states, work-study programs at 1,120 institutions, and 164 work-experience projects.[45]

In Washington and in the communities, the nation was aroused and quickly organized itself to participate in the new programs. However, after the second year, community action agency appropriations increased only moderately. As a result, the activities of many community action programs were confined to hiring a small staff and then applying for Head Start and one or two small additional components.[46]

Initially, OEO provided funds to community action agencies for program development and financing the cost of organizing and hiring staff. In many cases, the local community action agency was an administrative framework, and much of the money was funneled to the existing welfare agencies, such as the schools and the private agencies.

Although their existence indicated a dramatic change from the past, local community action agencies were not given complete freedom in the use of funds. Although the states initially did not have any control over the program, states eventually were given a technical assistance function and finally had a veto over program components. Regional OEO offices conducted several types of reviews. OEO employees personally carried on field reviews. There were personnel exchanges, orientation programs, and field trips by Washington personnel. A sample of Community Action Program applications were sent to Washington from the regional level for review for the purpose of quality control.[47]

Many local political leaders soon found the autonomous community action agencies a threat to their authority and control over local jobs. At times, the community action agencies threatened to upset traditional power relations in a community. Thus, national spokesmen for local governments continued to insist on the importance of the mayor in community action agency decisions. OEO tried to soothe both the community action agencies and local politicians. Eventually, community action agencies were forced by Congress to accept at least one-third of the members of the governing board appointed by City Hall. Furthermore, the local community action agency had to be the designate agency of city or state government.[48]

Once a new community action agency came into existence, there was a considerable time lag as they developed applications for grants. To speed up activity, OEO developed prepackaged national programs. Communities quickly recognized that Congress and OEO were pushing certain programs and that applications in these areas were likely to receive more expeditious treatment than programs that were created locally.[49] Also, national OEO started pushing national emphasis programs, programs that left less discretion to local agencies. As Levitan writes, "During OEO's first fiscal year, all CAP programs except Head Start were discretionary and presumably initiated locally. But by fiscal 1968, more than six of every ten CAP dollars were allocated to the national emphasis programs and other nationally directed efforts."[50] Over time, then, what started out as a block grant type of program, with an emphasis on local decision making, evolved into a conditional grant-in-aid type program with more federal control.

By the end of 1966, OEO began the process of cutting back the Community Action Program. "The one domestic program which President Johnson originally wanted most to make his own and which he launched so spectacularly in 1964 found itself two years later in serious difficulty in Congress, among the poor people it was designed to serve and, oddly enough, within the Executive Office of the President."[51] The reasons were many. The Vietnam War was taking the country's money, time, and attention. Community action brought political problems that should have been forseen, including the opposition of the cities' mayors. Congress, which had not been involved in initiating the program, had little stake in its perpetuation.[52]

In addition, there was a growing resistance, especially among whites, toward the program. A Harris public opinion poll taken in 1966 showed a dramatic decline in the support of the American people for the Poverty Program.[53]

OEO raised expectations that it had a difficult time fulfilling. According to Stephen M. Rose, in *The Betrayal of the Poor: The Transformation of Community Action,*[54] OEO was based on the wrong assumptions. Rose, among others,[55] suggests that there are alternative perspectives to the problem of poverty that can be arranged on a continuum. At one extreme, the individual is seen as responsible for his or her condition of poverty. Under this conception, Rose suggests that ". . . the condition of poverty is brought about by its inhabitants because of their own basic defects, deviant values, and/or immorality."[56] Poverty is seen as self-perpetuating and as a part of a subculture in American life. Policies based on this approach stress individual change and efforts to affect the culture of poverty. This is an individualistic perspective.

At the other extreme are humanitarian explanations that point to the structure of society as responsible for poverty. The economy (especially the free working of the market), discrimination, and other institutional factors produce poverty. Poor people are similar to middle-class and upper-class people except that they operate under institutional constraints that do not exist in the same degree for middle-class and upper-class individuals. Policies to eradicate poverty based on this conception have the goal of basic institutional change and major redistribution in the political and economic structures of the society. For Rose, the Community Action Program was based on the ". . . almost universal adoption of the Culture of Poverty ideal type, in the construction of programs based upon an individual and cultural change strategy, and in the perpetuation of poverty in America."[57]

Sar A. Levitan feels that the Poverty Program was a modern poor law.[58] Richard Titmus agrees. "In the Act and, in particular, the regulations under the Act, there is a curious affinity with the New Poor Law Act of 1834 in England. Both endorsed and legitimized prevailing social values, both believed in redemption through work regardless of whether work was available; both were rooted in pathological explanations of poverty."[59] For Levitan, poverty will continue as long as society grudgingly provides money for the poor. As the War on Poverty entered its third year, James Reston wrote, "The problem is defined: the programs all have vivid names; the machinery, new and still imperfect, is nevertheless in place; but the funds are lamentably inadequate to the gigantic scope of the problem."[60]

With a goal as difficult as eliminating poverty, the Poverty Program and its cornerstone, the Community Action Program, were seriously underfunded. As the country became more involved in the Vietnam War, guns replaced butter. Money and national attention and energy deserted the poor as quickly as concern originally had appeared. Critics charged that the Poverty Program was inadequate and ill conceived because it was based on the Poor Law approach of individual change through training and social services. Further, the Poverty Program raised expectations to unreasonable levels. However, with all these problems, jobs quickly were created for the poor in the program. After this initial opportunity, many would return to school and pursue jobs in the private sector. Further, the Community Action Program, with its emphasis on community participation, did seem to serve as a training ground for political leaders. It provided valuable experience for many individuals who would go on to compete successfully for local, state, and national political office. Finally, with all of its defects, the Poverty Program may have been one of the factors which made racial integration somewhat more acceptable in American society. While the country is still a long way from the goal of a racially integrated and harmonious society, we do seem to have made some progress. The Poverty Program might have been one of a series of factors—of which the Civil Rights Movement was probably the most important—which pushed the country toward beginning efforts at equal opportunity.

Earlier national efforts to help the poor were funded through a grant-in-aid type of approach characteristic of Cooperative Federalism. In contrast, the Community Action Program used the mechanism of the block grant typical of Creative Federalism. As Martha Derthick writes:

> If Creative Federalism is to be found in action, the most appropriate place to look for it may be in those grant programs that developed as the doctrine was being talked about. Model Cities was one, and another, two years earlier, was the Community Action Program of the War on Poverty. In many ways, this was the operational prototype of Creative Federalism. It incorporated the same stress on dispersing power and on coordinating diverse programs and institutions. . . . Through the medium of federal project grants, the fight against poverty became a local activity. And it was the Community Action Program, with its provision of maximum feasible participation of those affected, that made citizen participation an ideological issue, and thus a new article of liberal faith.[61]

The Community Action Program represents a heavy reliance by the federal government on local planning agencies for a specific purpose. This aspect of Creative Federalism was repeated in another program, Model Cities. But whereas the Community Action Program emphasized community participation and the establishment of community action agencies outside of city government in order to accomplish a nationally established goal, Model Cities attempted a more rational, planned approach to help low-income persons, with operating control located in City Hall itself.

MODEL CITIES

Model Cities was authorized by Title I of the Demonstration Cities and Metropolitan Development Act of 1966 (Public Law

89-794). Its purpose was to concentrate on the social, economic, and physical problems of slum and blighted neighborhoods. Model Cities attempted to join social and physical planning for a comprehensive, five-year attack on specific geographical sections of the cities. In contrast to the Poverty Program, responsibility was located in City Hall. In part, its purpose was to ". . . further develop the capability of local government to deal with city-wide problems similar to those faced in model neighborhood areas."[62]

For the first three years of the program, Congress appropriated $23 million for planning grants to cities, $512.5 million for supplemental grants, and $412.5 million for urban renewal projects in the model neighborhoods.[63]

Model Cities planning grants covered 80 percent of the approved cost of planning a program. Grants were appropriated on the basis of population, along with a consideration of the relative seriousness of social, physical, and economic problems.[64]

Model Cities was a program of the U.S. Department of Housing and Urban Development (HUD). Consistent with Creative Federalism, it emphasized community determination of the means to implement the federally established objectives. As HUD Secretary Robert Weaver said, "This is a local program. It will be planned, developed, and carried out by local people."[65]

In order to implement the program, cities established City Demonstration Agencies (CDA) that were responsible to the chief executive, often the mayor. HUD guidelines emphasized the use of the planning process.

According to HUD's "Comprehensive Program Submission Requirements,"[66] there were three major phases of the Model Cities Program, all of which involved extensive planning. In the first phase, cities prepared a Planning Grant Application. This application described in detail the social, economic, and physical problems of the area selected for the Model Cities Program. Cities developed goals related to the broad problems and established priorities among these goals. The Planning Grant Application also included specific programs to meet these goals and associated strategies to develop the programs. Finally, there was a description of the administrative machinery that was envisioned to implement the plan. In contrast to the Community Action Program, the Grant Application for Model Cities involved a substantial investment by cities before they received their funds. Much of this was carried on by planners or consultants and did not involve broad community participation.

If a city was successful and its Grant Application was approved, they had one year to refine the planning grant proposal. The machinery to implement a five-year program was to be established during the first-year planning grant. Specific proposals were to be developed in the areas of physical improvement, housing, health, education, employment, recreation, crime reduction, and social services. For each area, there was to be a description of the need, the city's present effort, the goals, and the program approach. The first-year plan had to include a description of who would carry out the various programs. Finally, provision for evaluation of the results was required.[67]

When the plan was approved, cities were given monies for implementation. These federal monies, distributed through the Department of Housing and Urban Development, could be used as the local share to attract conditional grants-in-aid from other federal departments. Cities often used their Model Cities operating grants to attract substantially larger grants from other federal departments.

The Model Cities Program contains many of the elements of programs developed under Creative Federalism. Like the Community Action Program, there were nationally established goals. These goals insured that Model Cities would be geared to serve low-income neighborhoods. Also, there was some freedom on the local level to determine the programmatic means to implement these goals.

However, Model Cities was different from the Community Action Program in several important respects. In the first place, the Community Action Program was operated locally through a newly created community agency established outside of City Hall. In contrast, Model Cities, on the local level, could be controlled directly by the mayor or his assistants.

The Community Action Program covered a wider geographic area. In order not to repeat the abuses that occurred under the Urban Renewal Program, where whole neighborhoods were destroyed, Model Cities Programs could be located only in low-income neighborhoods where there was some adequate housing. Cities were strictly prohibited from clearing off large tracts, although clearance and rehabilitation of individual deteriorated houses was encouraged. Whereas the Community Action Program was for all individuals who lived in poor neighborhoods, Model Cities usually was restricted to certain of these neighborhoods.

Finally, where the Community Action Program emphasized community and neighborhood participation, Model Cities attempted to develop a more rational, planned approach to change. Although residents and other actors were still involved in Model Cities, the fact of City Hall control and the nature of the elaborate planning process placed a greater emphasis on decisions either by experts and/or, depending on the city, by political appointees of the mayor. To a greater extent than under the Community Action Program, the preplanning and planning process under Model Cities was removed from the arena of broad community decision making and confined to a smaller decision making group that often included technical experts and City Hall appointees.

Model Cities was an effort to apply sophisticated management techniques to social change in the Model Cities neighborhood. In addition, since it was funded through City Hall, Model Cities was an effort to co-op the bureaucracy and make it more responsive to areas of the city which had been ignored. The goal of Model Cities was nothing short of the social, economic, and physical revival of a part of the city characterized by serious problems. This revival was to be accomplished through the intervention of a previously unresponsive bureaucracy. Model Cities failed miserably in both of these lofty goals. In many cities, Model Cities was a patchwork of individual programs which were selected for a variety of reasons. Some were supported because they benefited a present or potential friend of the Mayor or his associates. Other programs were selected because they brought a lot of federal money into the city through the use of Model Cities money as a local share for other conditional grants-in-aid. Like the Poverty Program, which it was designed to control, if not replace, Model Cities was underfinanced. Perhaps as important, Model Cities suffered from a lack of skill at the city level. Political appointees often were involved in making complex decisions about housing, social services, and employment. They often did not have expertise in these areas or an ability to engage in a planning process whose goal was community improvement.

Model Cities also suffered from some of the inherent conflicts of social planning in a democracy which had been evident in the Grey Areas Projects. Rational decision making, which implies some degree of centralization and control by experts, was in conflict with interest group politics. In other words, even the best developed plans could be defeated by urban political realities.

The Poverty Program still remains in most American cities, albeit in changed form. Model Cities was merged at the municipal level into a new block grant. This new program, which established local Community Development Agencies, was developed during the Nixon years. Its purpose was to combine several similar housing and urban development programs into one group and allow substantial local control. The disappointing legacy of Model Cities was that comprehensive planning engineered through City Hall did not work to the advantage of poor communities.

Conclusion

The Creative Federalism of Lyndon Johnson and John Kennedy was a first step at consolidating the proliferating grants of earlier administrations. More community decision making and planning, direct federal–city funding of programs, and participation of those affected by the programs were the hallmarks of many of the newer programs, including the Community Action Program and Model Cities.

The goals of Creative Federalism were, on the one hand, to consolidate, coordinate, and rationalize the mammoth federal grant-in-aid structure. A second purpose was decentralization, both to lower levels of government and to the people themselves. The growing power and influence of Washington had to be limited.[68]

Model Cities included some of the aspects of Creative Federalism. In the beginning, it was a block grant program, with localities free to choose the means to implement federal goals. Model Cities attempted to decentralize power to the municipal level, but the nature of the planning process, which was often quite technical and political, did not lend itself to participation by neighborhood groups and by citizens as much as community action did. Since Model Cities funds could be used as matching money to attract other federal conditional grant-in-aids, cities soon learned which federal grants had the most desirable funding formulas. With the help of the Department of Housing and Urban Renewal, which reviewed the total process, there was some encouragement for cities to develop certain programs and not others. For example, several cities developed income maintenance experiments, but only a few were approved by HUD.

Like the Community Action Program, what started out as a block grant with total local control in the selection of means resulted in a program in which federal officials were involved both in the selection of goals and the determination of means.

Model Cities and other similarly structured programs led to pressure for more community decision making.

Creative Federalism was a reaction against the past. Cooperative Federalism had resulted in greater federal power. Roger H. Davidson wrote that "Many in the Administration's team which drafted the (anti-poverty) bill harbored a deep antipathy toward the traditional grant-in-aid, in which federal funds were administered by the states under specified conditions."[69] But Creative Federalism did not go far enough in returning power to the local communities. It was up to the Republicans to press this objective in the Revenue Sharing Program, under the New Federalism.

NOTES

1. *City of Clinton* vs. *Cedar Rapids and Missouri River Railroad Company,* 24 Iowa 455 (1868).

2. Roscoe C. Martin. *The Cities and the Federal System.* New York: Atherton Press, 1965.

3. James L. Sundquist, with the collaboration of David W. Davis. *Making Federalism Work: A Study of Program Coordination at the Community Level.* Washington, D.C.: The Brookings Institution, 1969, p. 1.

4. Francis Fox Piven and Richard A. Cloward. *Regulating the Poor: The Functions of Public Welfare.* New York: Pantheon Books, 1971.

5. James Sundquist. *Politics and Policy: The Eisenhower, Kennedy, and Johnson Years.* Washington, D.C.: The Brookings Institution, 1968, pp. 389–537.

6. Peter Marris and Martin Rein. *Dilemmas of Social Reform: Poverty and Community Action in the United States.* New York: Atherton Press, 1969, pp. 1–12.

7. Sundquist and Davis, pp. 389–537.

8. Sundquist, p. 111.

9. Sundquist and Davis, p. 1.

10. Michael Reagan. *The New Federalism.* New York: Oxford University Press, 1972, p. 28.

11. Ibid.

12. Gilbert Steiner. *The State of Welfare.* Washington, D.C.: The Brookings Institution, 1971, p. 147.

13. Sundquist and Davis, p. 25.

14. Martha Derthick. *The Influence of Federal Grants: Public Assistance in Massachusetts.* Cambridge: Harvard University Press, 1970, p. 224.

15. Subcommittee on Intergovernmental Relations, Committee on Governmental Operation, U.S. Senate, *Creative Federalism,* 89th Congress, 2nd Session, 1966, Part I, p. 268.

16. Ibid., p. 269.

17. Richard Goodwin. "The Shape of American Politics," *Commentary,* 5, June 1967, 36.

18. Marris and Rein, p. 14–32.

19. Ibid.

20. Lloyd Ohlin and Richard Cloward. *Delinquency and Opportunity.* Glencoe, Ill.: Free Press, 1960.

21. Ibid.

22. Marris and Rein.

23. Ibid.

24. Ibid., pp. 224–238.

25. Sar A. Levitan. *The Great Society's Poor Law: A New Approach to Poverty.* Baltimore: Johns Hopkins Press, 1969.

26. Robert J. Lampman. "The Low Income Population and Economic Growth." Joint Economic Committee, Congress of the United States, 86th Congress, 1st Session. Washington, D.C.: U.S. Government Printing Office, December 16, 1959.

27. Levitan.

28. Michael Harrington. *The Other America: Poverty in the United States.* Baltimore: Penguin Books, 1962.

29. John C. Donovan. *The Politics of Poverty.* New York: Pegasus, 1967, p. 26.

30. Ibid.

31. Robert H. Haverman. "Poverty, Income Distribution, and Social Policy: The Last Decade and the Next." *Public Policy, 25* (1), Winter 1977.

32. Levitan, p. 18.

33. Ibid., p. 20.

34. Donovan, p. 61.

35. Paul E. Peterson and J. David Greenstone. "Racial Change and Participation: The Mobilization of Low-Income Communities Through Community Action." In Robert H. Haverman, Ed., *A Decade of Federal Antipoverty Programs: Achievements, Failures, and Lessons.* New York: Academic Press, 1978.

36. Sundquist, pp. 137–145.

37. Levitan, p. 52.

38. Daniel Moynihan. "What Is Community Action?" *Public Interest,* Fall 1966, p. 6.

39. Levitan, p. 121.

40. Ibid., pp. 30–31.

41. Ibid., p. 163.

42. Public Law 88–452, 88th Congress, S. 2642, August 20, 1964.

43. Ibid.

44. Ibid., p. 9.

45. Office of Economic Opportunity. *A Nation Aroused: First Annual Report.* Washington, D.C.: 1965.

46. Levitan, p. 122.

47. Levitan, p. 121.

48. Ibid. pp. 63–67.

49. Ibid., p. 122.

50. Ibid., p. 124.

51. Donovan, p. 80.

52. Ibid.

53. Sundquist, p. 497.

54. Stephen M. Rose. *The Betrayal of the Poor: The Transformation of Community Action.* Cambridge, Mass.: Schenkman Publishing, 1972.

55. For example, S. M. Miller and Frank Reissman. *Social Class and Social Policy.* New York: Basic Books, 1968; David G. Gil. *Unravelling Social Policy: Theory, Analysis, and Political Action Towards Social Equality.* Cambridge, Mass.: Schenkman Publishing, 1973; S. M. Miller and Pamela Roby. *The Future of Inequality.* New York: Basic Books, 1970.

56. Ibid., p. 3.

57. Rose, p. 174.

58. Levitan, p. 318.

59. Richard Titmus. *Essays on the Welfare State.* New Haven, Conn.: Yale University Press, 1959, p. 113.

60. James Reston. *New York Times,* March 15, 1967.

61. Derthick, pp. 224–225.

62. U.S. Department of Housing and Urban Development, "The Model Cities Program, Questions and Answers." Washington, D.C.: U.S. Government Printing Office, January 1970, p. 1.

63. Ibid.

64. Ibid., p. 25.

65. U.S. Department of Housing and Urban Development, "History of Congressional Action Relative to Model Cities, 1966–1967," n.d., p. 33.

66. U.S. Department of Housing and Urban Development, "Comprehensive Program Submission Requirements." Washington, D.C.: U.S. Department of Housing and Urban Development, July 1968.

67. Ibid.

68. Derthick, p. 235.

69. Roger Davidson. "Creative Federalism and the War on Poverty." *Poverty and Human Resource Abstracts 1,* November–December 1966, 5–14.

Chapter 5

NEW FEDERALISM

INTRODUCTION

When Richard Nixon became President, one of his major goals
was to continue the trend to decentralize federal power started
under Creative Federalism. Basic to the New Federalism of
Richard Nixon was returning power and decision-making authority in the area of domestic policy to the community level.
General Revenue Sharing was a major program of the New
Federalism. General Revenue Sharing was enacted in 1972 as
the State and Local Fiscal Assistance Act of 1972.

Nixon was also hostile toward social welfare. During his
administration, a major effort was made to dismantle the Poverty Program. Nixon successfully destroyed Model Cities by
merging it into a new block grant in the area of housing and
urban development. The effort to decentralize decision making
through the General Revenue Sharing Program was consistent
with this philosophy since social welfare interests are generally
least powerful on the community level.

During the first five years of operation, General Revenue Sharing provided $30.2 billion to general-purpose governments (states, counties, municipalities, townships, and Indian Tribal Councils). Money collected by the federal government was regularly sent to general-purpose governments to be spent for a wide variety of government functions, including social services for the poor and aged.

General Revenue Sharing is structured differently from other federal programs, such as conditional grants-in-aid and block grants. Under conditional grant-in-aid programs, the federal government provides money to states and localities for specific purposes. The ways in which monies can be spent also are prescribed. The conditional grant-in-aid program involves the greatest amount of federal participation. Many programs under the Poverty Program developed numerous characteristics of the grant-in-aid.

Under a block grant program, the federal government establishes goals and objectives and provides states and localities with a "block" of money. Here, there is more freedom on the community level to determine the means (i.e., programs) to be employed to implement federal objectives. Block grant-type programs involve less federal control than conditional grants-in-aid and more control than General Revenue Sharing. Under General Revenue Sharing, there was virtually no federal control.

RATIONALE FOR GENERAL REVENUE SHARING

Richard Nathan has suggested the following rationale as the most frequently cited justifications for adopting General Revenue Sharing:

> To help meet domestic public needs at the state and local level.
>
> To stabilize or reduce state and local taxes, particularly the property tax.

To decentralize government.

To equalize fiscal conditions between rich and poor states and localities.

To alter the nation's overall tax system by placing greater reliance on income taxation (predominantly federal) as opposed to property and sales taxation.[1]

In addition, it was felt that General Revenue Sharing would reduce the size and importance of the federal conditional grant-in-aid program. In fact, during the first years of operation, General Revenue Sharing accounted for almost 25 percent of the total federal grants to state and local governments.[2]

Concern about how to pay for public services on the state and local levels was a major factor that led to the development of General Revenue Sharing. With the exception of Social Security, veterans' benefits, and farmers' subsidies, state and local governments deliver almost all public services. Although there has been increased pressure on the local level for more and better services, raising money is more difficult on the local level. State and local taxes are generally inflexible, regressive, and the poor states are at a disadvantage. Under state and local taxation, poor and middle-income people pay a larger percentage of their income for taxes than do the wealthy. On the other hand, federal taxes have been flexible and mildly progressive.

Of the three major types of taxes, the income tax is used primarily by the federal government. The income tax is the most progressive tax; richer Americans generally pay a higher percentage of their income than poorer Americans. Sales and property taxes are generally regressive taxes. The general sales tax is the primary source of money for the states. The property tax is the primary source of funds for localities.

Of these taxes, the income tax has the greatest degree of elasticity. In other words, there is the greatest fluctuation in revenue because of economic conditions. Given an average rate of growth of the Gross National Product (GNP), the federal government increases its tax revenues by \$6 to \$7 billion annually, without having to legislate any new taxes. In comparison, the cigarette tax, a type of sales tax, rises only 40 percent as fast as incomes, and the property tax has an elasticity of 1.0, or a yield proportionate to economic growth.[3]

The attributes of these taxes are reflected in the amount of the total tax dollars collected by each level of government. For example, in 1968, the federal government collected 62 percent of all public revenues, the states, 26 percent, and local government, 12 percent. As much as people talk about pure federalism, it is clear that the federal government, with its superior tax system and fiscal ability, is in a position to exert the strongest degree of control.[4]

The prospects for the future do not indicate a change in this trend. For example, Congressman Henry R. Reuss of Wisconsin, Chairman of the House Banking Committee, feels that state and local governments are unlikely to raise enough money to meet their needs in the next decade, and their doing so would be "economically dangerous, socially undesirable, and politically improbable, since state-local taxes, as opposed to federal taxes, tend to be inequitable and inflexible."[5]

General Revenue Sharing was also developed because of pressure to reverse the growing power and inefficiency of the federal government. This concern had started during Creative Federalism and reached its height during the New Federalism. Men such as Walter Heller, John Gardner, and Richard Goodwin were interested in decentralization as a way to increase the administrative capabilities of state and local government. However, their perspective was a national perspective. As Heller wrote in proposing his Revenue Sharing Plan:

> the federal government simply cannot carry out large segments of its responsibilities at all—or all efficiently—without strengthening the states and localities. . . . States and localities . . . will continue to be the service centers through which important national purposes are achieved. If we don't want these purposes

thwarted or diluted, we had better strengthen those operating units.[6]

Humanitarians like Heller felt that there were countervailing forces that would insure that states and localities would use money under revenue sharing for the "right" purposes. The first was reapportionment, which moved more in the direction of "one man, one vote." Furthermore, humanitarians hoped that the increased emphasis throughout the nation on citizen participation in local governmental decisions would insure the accountability of local officials. Finally, with the provision of federal monies, state and local governments would not be forced to pay a political price by raising taxes in order to increase public services. By using the "free money" provided by the federal government, state and local governments would not be hampered by political constraints, and the money could be used in the public interest.

However, there are several factors that may work against this direction. The first is that, as Martha Derthick suggests, there is some indication that political outcomes are more humanitarian as the decision making unit increases in scale.[7] Under this hypothesis, humanitarian outcomes increase the higher one goes in government. To the extent that this is true, local revenue sharing monies would not be spent for the kinds of projects Heller seemed to be imagining when he proposed the idea. This is true in part because interest groups, which tend to have humanitarian purposes, such as labor unions and minority groups, have more power on the national level. Rural and suburban interest groups, which have a more individualistic orientation, have been strong supporters of the revenue sharing approach.[8]

The trend toward increased local control was viewed with suspicion by many concerned with social welfare services. Writing about General Revenue Sharing in the summer of 1972, several months before its passage, Gerald Wheeler wrote that "Localism has consistently worked against the poor and minority groups. If undue power is concentrated in Washington, it has become so as the only feasible alternative available in the attempt to secure membership of America's disadvantaged and disenfranchised groups in the larger society. . . . If the destiny of Americans . . . is transferred to state and local governments, the end result will be to turn back history with respect to human welfare."[9]

A similar position was put forth by Wilbur Cohen, a past Secretary of the U.S. Department of Health, Education and Welfare. Cohen wrote, "We have to have federal programs with strings attached because it is the only way that the disadvantaged, the poor whites and poor blacks will get their fair share. If there are not federally regulated programs to disburse money and instead it is handled by local city governments, then they won't get their fair share."[10]

General Revenue Sharing emphasizes municipal control of both the purposes and the means for implementing these purposes. In contrast to conditional grant-in-aid and block grant programs, there is almost no federal supervision of the use of federal monies.

Specifically, General Revenue Sharing can be distinguished from grant-in-aid and block grant programs, which have:

Required extensive planning and application efforts on the part of participant governments.

Required periodic reporting and reapplication in order to continue to receive funds.

Limited participation to a subgroup of all governments applying, with the selection of participants based on "need" and the program applications.

Required a cash or in-kind match from participating units.

Limited program areas to those that reflected nationally determined priorities.

Been subject to annual review by Congress and the federal executive branch.[11]

HISTORY OF GENERAL REVENUE SHARING

Since the 1930s, extension of federal responsibility has been primarily associated with the Democratic party. Republicans attacked enlarging federal responsibility and called it socialism. Representing the individualistic perspective, Republicans thought that the extension of federal power would result in the weakening of the power of local government and, therefore, of individual freedom. President Eisenhower started the movement toward more decentralization with the Commission on Intergovernmental Relations. In a dissenting opinion, the final report of the Commission took issue with its original charge, rejecting the idea that the extension of the federal government was an usurpation of states' rights. "The national government and the states should be regarded not as competitors for authority but as two levels of government cooperating with or complementing each other in meeting the growing demands on both."[12]

However, the thrust for decentralization continued, at first in the thinking of policy advisors. A radical idea was suggested by Walter Heller, past chairman of the Council of Economic Advisors. Heller proposed that the federal government allocate to state and local governments 1 to 2 percent of the federal individual income tax with "next to no strings attached."[13] In retrospect, Derthick feels that "the Heller proposal for revenue sharing, alone among the ideas developed, represented a significant departure from the grant system, and, though considered by the administration and promoted by Republicans in Congress, it was not adopted."[14]

Melvin Laird was one of the earliest Republican advocates of revenue sharing. Laird's interest in the proposal started when he was a member of the 1946 Wisconsin Legislature, which passed a state revenue sharing plan. In 1958, as a Republican congressman from Wisconsin, Laird introduced into the national House of Representatives a bill calling for tax sharing legislation that included a 5 percent rebate to the states of federally collected revenues.

In 1960, Walter Heller proposed that 1 to 2 percent of the receipts of the federal income tax be returned to the states every year. Heller suggested that a trust fund be established to emphasize the fact that the states would receive money as a right. The use of a trust fund would insure that revenue sharing monies would be separate from and not encroach on federal conditional grant-in-aid programs. Heller felt that the most important result of revenue sharing would be to revitalize the states and localities. In 1968, Heller revised his plan to allow for a pass-through provision to localities. According to David Caputo and Richard Cole, the Heller plan was enormously influential, and many of its original components were included in the final bill.[15]

In 1964, the Democratic party at its National Convention included in its platform a proposal that the federal government should consider the development of a program to share monies with the states and localities. In his presidential campaign that year, President Johnson supported the concept and said that the federal government should make some part of the federal tax revenues, over and above existing aids, available to the states and localities.[16]

After becoming President, Johnson appointed a task force on revenue sharing headed by Joseph A. Pechman of the Brookings Institution. Walter Heller assisted Pechman. The task force recommended that 2 percent of federal revenues be distributed to the states yearly, based on an allocation formula including population, tax effort, and income. In 1968, the National Commission on Urban Problems, appointed by President Johnson and chaired by Senator Paul H. Douglas, recommended that revenue sharing be enacted to ease the financial crisis of the major cities.[17]

Earlier, in 1966, Republican Congressman Charles E. Goodell of New York introduced to the House of Representatives a revenue sharing proposal. The distribution formula favored the less wealthy states, and there was a pass-through provision so that localities would also receive money. The Republican party supported the revenue sharing concept in 1966 in a report of the Republican Coordinating Committee entitled "Financing the Future of Federalism: The Case for Revenue Sharing."[18]

Caputo and Cole write that revenue sharing had gained substantial intellectual, political and public support by the time Richard M. Nixon had gained the Republican Party's nomination for President of the United States in 1968.[19] A Gallup poll in 1967 showed 70 percent of the population in favor of the idea. President-elect Nixon appointed Richard Nathan to head an intergovernmental task force whose final report favored revenue sharing. Arthur Burns, Nixon's chief economic advisor, appointed a revenue sharing task force in 1969 that recommended the Heller-Pechman approach. Nixon's revenue sharing proposal was introduced in September 1969 by Senator Howard Baker and was a key element of the President's New Federalism.[20]

During the late 1960s there was considerable intellectual reaction against the centralization of the federal government. Caputo and Cole suggest that several important books and articles helped to create an intellectual rationale for decentralization. These writings include Peter F. Drucker's *Age of Discontinuity,*[21] Daniel Moynihan's *Maximum Feasible Misunderstanding,*[22] James Sundquist and David Davis' *Making Federalism Work,*[23] Edward Banfield's *The Unheavenly City,*[24] and Richard Goodwin's article entitled "The Shape of American Politics."[25]

No congressional hearings were held on the revenue sharing bill during the 1969 to 1970 session, and the administration stepped up pressure for passage. Richard Nathan and Associates report that the Secretary of the Treasury Department, the National League of Cities, the U.S. Conference of Mayors, the National Governor's Conference, the Council of State Governments, the International City Manager's Association, and the National Association of Counties pressured Congress for a Revenue Sharing Bill.[26]

In his State of the Union Message in 1971, President Nixon said, "The time has now come in America to reverse the flow of power and resources from the states and communities to Washington, and start power and resources flowing back . . . to the states and communities and, more important, to the people all across America."

The revenue sharing proposal came to Congress in two parts. The first included the establishment of a permanent general revenue sharing fund that would distribute a fixed percentage of federal tax receipts. Monies from it were to be distributed to state and local governments with virtually no conditions attached. The fund eventually was eliminated by Congress, although the initial appropriation was for a five-year period. The second part of the proposal established what has been called special revenue sharing. It used the block grant approach and consolidated 130 conditional grants-in-aid into six areas to deal with urban community development, rural community development, manpower training, education, law enforcement, and transportation. There was resistance in Congress to many of the special revenue sharing programs, since they turned more control over to state and local officials and they eliminated many beneficial conditional grant-in-aid programs. However, Congress passed the Comprehensive Employment and Training Act of 1973 and the Community Development Act of 1974. In addition, legislation in the area of education and law enforcement (LEAA) incorporated some of the ideas of the original special revenue sharing proposals.

According to Wallace Oates, Congressman Wilbur Mills, Chairman of the powerful House Ways and Means Committee was an early opponent of General Revenue Sharing. Although a long time supporter of states rights, Mills opposed the weakening of federal direction and control. He also objected to the original formula proposed to distribute the revenue sharing money. Oates writes that Mills was able to change the distribution formula so that it included, in addition to the provisions of population size and tax effort, the provision of the relative size of the urbanized population and the level of per capita income. Mills also felt that the level of government that spent taxes should be responsible for their collection. He identified the seven high-priority areas for local governmental expenditures, thus providing some federal direction, although no effective control, over the monies. The House of Representatives refused to establish a trust fund, as had been proposed by the Nixon administration. The House did appropriate monies for five years, thus avoiding annual review of the program.

The Senate developed its own formula for the distribution of the monies, and the final bill included both House and Senate formulas, with states using the formula that would be most beneficial to them.[27]

A joint conference committee worked on developing agreement around different distribution formulas. The House accepted the conference report on October 12, 1972, the Senate, one day later. President Nixon signed the State and Local Fiscal Assistance Act into law on October 20, 1972.

When revenue sharing was first considered in the 1960s, it was viewed as one approach to stimulate the economy. Walter Heller wrote of the "fiscal drag" on the economy that slowed down private production when federal revenues exceeded expenditures. Since a federal revenue surplus was undesirable, fiscal drag could be overcome by "fiscal dividends"—a tax cut or the expansion of programs, for example, through revenue sharing.[28]

However, by the time revenue sharing was finally enacted, the country faced the opposite problem. The federal budget surplus of the 1960s had vanished and a situation of scarcity existed. Revenue sharing went into effect at the same time that the Nixon administration, in its proposed budget for 1974, announced important and, in many cases, deep cuts in federal domestic spending. In some cases, money allocated by Congress was impounded, or not spent by the administration. This created a "pincer effect" (i.e., the simultaneous occurrence of revenue sharing and threatened domestic budget cuts created more interest in state and local budgeting). Interest groups on the local level could pressure officials to offset the federal budget cuts with revenue sharing monies.[29]

GENERAL REVENUE SHARING IN OPERATION—EFFECTS OF THE DISTRIBUTION FORMULAS

One of the two formulas was used in determining a state's share of General Revenue Sharing funds. Tax effort was an important component of each formula and was calculated yearly. Population and income, based on the 1970 Census, were also included in the formula. The formulas favor states that had a high tax effort.[30]

One-third of the state's total General Revenue Sharing funds was allocated to the state government, with the remaining two-thirds available to the states' local governments. This was allocated first to county areas using a formula that takes into account each county's population, relative income, and general tax effort. The act contained limitations on the amounts allocated to local governments. The per capita amount may not be less than 20 percent or more than 145 percent of the per capita amount available for distribution throughout the state. Furthermore, a local government's allocation may not exceed 50 percent of the sum of adjusted taxes and intergovernmental transfers received by a local government. There were 38,873 eligible recipients in the United States.[31]

When revenue sharing funds are compared to the scale of local governments existing before revenue sharing, large metropolitan areas, while benefiting, benefit to a much lesser degree than their suburbs. ". . . The program's benefits as so measured generally are less for local governments in metropolitan areas, for those in large and densely populated counties, and for large-population municipalities than for the appropriate counterpart groups or jurisdictions."[32]

According to Richard Nathan and Associates,

... the distribution of shared revenue can be expected, by and large, to permit relatively more easing of local taxes (or more expansion of local government expenditure) in thinly populated areas whose per capita levels of taxation and financing are below average than in more urbanized, higher-cost areas. . . .[33]

Local governments may use revenue sharing funds for priority expenses that the act defines as (1) ordinary and necessary capital expenditures authorized by law, and (2) operating and maintenance expenses for public safety, environmental protection, public transportation, health, recreation, libraries, social services for the poor and aged, and financial administration. Local governments were to meet equal opportunity requirements with their revenue sharing monies and publish annually an actual use report of how they spent their revenue sharing funds.[34]

Social services money could not be spent for public welfare grants. Examples of acceptable social service expenditures were operating and maintaining public housing, nursing and old age homes, neighborhood social centers, and youth employment programs that hire poor youths or help them get employment. In a clarification of this category from the Office of Revenue Sharing, U.S. Department of the Treasury, the cost of administrating a food stamp program or a community action program was acceptable. The administration of a program, only part of which benefits the poor, was not acceptable.[35]

Several observers have tried to make the case that the expenditures for social services were larger than those reported on the actual use forms. In testimony before the Senate Committee on Governmental Operations, Mayor Moon Landrieu of New Orleans, representing the National League of Cities and the U.S. Conference of Mayors, said that "Many programs that fall under the other seven priority categories serve the poor and the elderly in our communities. Taking this more comprehensive definition, a far greater percentage of revenue sharing money is being spent for our less advantaged citizens than has been reported by ORS (Office of Revenue Sharing)."[36]

ALLOCATIONS OF GENERAL REVENUE SHARING MONIES ON THE MUNICIPAL LEVEL

There have been numerous studies of revenue sharing that attempt to determine the effect of the program on municipal expenditure patterns. The major research method has been to study the Actual Use Reports. Some scholars have also created models of local budgeting patterns over time, in order to determine the effect of revenue sharing.

The Actual Use Reports, which each city is required to publish describing its yearly revenue sharing allocations by function, appear to be a useful tool for social scientists. However (because of the problem of fungibility) these reports can be misleading in terms of the actual expenditure of funds. This confusion can occur because, with so few controls attached to the program on the local level, money initially allocated for a particular purpose may eventually, in fact, be used for a different purpose. For example, a General Revenue Sharing allocation of a given amount of money by a locality to the police department may increase the normal budget of the department. However, this revenue sharing allocation may free up (or displace) the same amount of money, obtained from a different revenue source. The displaced money now can be allocated to another program. As this example shows, the addition of the revenue sharing money to a particular department does not necessarily yield a net increase in the department's budget. Also, the money can be substituted for other sources of revenue, thus allowing a cut in revenue requirements from these other sources.[37] As Richard Nathan and Associates write, "Revenue sharing funds are not radioactive; they can be extremely difficult to trace."[38] However, in the area of social services, the amount of money allocated is similar to the amount spent.

David Caputo and Richard Cole published one of the earliest studies of revenue sharing allocations in the *Municipal Yearbook*. Using the Actual Use Reports, they found, during the initial period, only 1.6 percent of the funds were allocated for social services for the poor and aged. These allocations for social services occurred predominantly in Western cities. Mayor-council operated cities made more social service allocations than did council-manager or commission cities. Allocations for social services were somewhat more characteristic of partisan-type cities (where local candidates ran for office from an identified political party) as compared to nonpartisan-type cities.[39]

The Comptroller General has made regular studies of local revenue sharing allocations based on the Actual Use Reports. In 1974, a report was issued on allocations by 250 local governments. It described the use of $1.7 billion distributed to these governments through June 30, 1973. When social services for the poor and aged are considered, counties designated 10.3 percent of their funds and cities 2 percent of their funds for this purpose.[40] A year later, a study of 26 selected cities indicated little change in this pattern. The cities reported 3 percent of their operating funds and 1 percent of their capital acquisition and construction funds for social services for the poor and aged.[41] A study by the Office of Revenue Sharing, Department of the Treasury, based on Actual Use Reports from July 1, 1973 to June 30, 1974, showed similar results. When all local governments are considered ($N = 34,487$), 2 percent of the total fund went for social services. This includes allocations of $112.6 million for operating and capital expenses. When only city governments are considered for the same entitlement period ($N = 16,763$), of those reporting, 1 percent of the funds went for social services, or $35.3 million for both operating and capital expenses.[42]

In comparisons of allocations for 1973 and 1974 for all jurisdictions, Caputo and Cole found a higher allocation for social services during 1974. In general, they found that reported expenditures have been concentrated in the areas of law enforcement, fire prevention, environmental protection, street and road repair, and parks and recreation. Increasing size was directly associated with reported expenditures for police and fire protection. City type did not affect allocation decisions, although for social services there was a slightly higher percentage allocation in suburban areas than in central cities. Mayor-council cities spent a higher percentage for police and fire, while council-manager cities reported a higher percentage for parks and recreation.[43]

Thomas J. Anton and Associates attempted to discover the actual instead of reported use of revenue sharing funds. Since revenue sharing funds are given to city governments that have established financing patterns, ". . . the research problem is not to trace particular dollars from receipt to disbursement, but to discover changes in disbursement patterns over time which result from the availability of additional funds."[44] The approach is to attempt to determine the fiscal effects of revenue sharing, or the difference between the pattern that would have resulted without revenue sharing money and the pattern that developed with it.

Anton and Associates developed models based on different assumptions about how cities budget their money. In order to determine the extent to which each model replicated real outcomes, revenue and expenditure data were collected for five cities over a 17 to 23-year period (Albuquerque, New Mexico; Ann Arbor, Michigan; Cincinnati, Ohio; Detroit, Michigan; and Worcester, Massachusetts).

When the model selected is compared to the stated Actual Use Reports of the governments, there are two dramatic results. The category of General Government is significantly under-reported in the Actual Use Reports as compared to the actual expenditures. The five cities reported to the Office of Revenue Sharing that only 0.9 percent of their monies were allocated to this category, while Anton found that 43 percent of the revenue sharing monies actually ended up in this category. On the other hand, expenditures for public safety seemed to be overreported to the public. Anton finds that 42.2 percent of the revenue sharing funds were actually spent on this function, while the cities reported 79.05 percent of their funds were spent on public safety. There was minimal change in the social service category with cities reporting 0.6 percent of their funds in this area and Anton finding an actual allocation of 1.7 percent ($1,407,200) for social services.[45]

CONCLUSION

In conclusion, General Revenue Sharing is a program that operates under almost no federal constraints. In contrast to the Community Action Program and Model Cities, where federal programmatic goals have been established, allocations for programs under revenue sharing depend entirely on the local municipal decision making process. Under this situation, only a small percentage of the total money available—around 2 percent—is allocated for social services for the poor and aged.

Considering this trend toward greater municipal decision making, it is important to identify the community factors that can maximize allocations for social welfare. Part II describes an empirical study that identifies these factors under varying degrees of federal control.

NOTES

1. Richard P. Nathan. "Statement on Revenue Sharing," Senate Subcommittee on Intergovernmental Relations, June 5, 1974, p. 4.

2. Morton H. Sklar. "The Impact of Revenue Sharing on Minorities and the Poor." *Harvard Civil Rights Civil Liberties Law Review,* January 1975, 103.

3. Michael Reagan. *The New Federalism.* New York: Oxford University Press, 1972, pp. 37–38.

4. Ibid.

5. Henry R. Reuss. *Revenue Sharing: Crutch or Catalyst for State and Local Governments.* New York: Praeger, 1970, p. 25.

6. Walter Heller. *New Dimensions of Political Economy.* Cambridge, Mass.: Harvard University Press, 1966, pp. 123–124.

7. Derthick, p. 224.

8. Jeffrey L. Pressman. "Political Implications of the New Federalism." In Robert P. Inman, Martin McGuire, Wallace E. Oates, Jeffrey L. Pressman, and Robert D. Reischauer. *Financing the New Federalism: Revenue Sharing, Conditional Grants, and Taxation.* Baltimore: Johns Hopkins University Press, 1975, pp. 13–39.

9. Gerald R. Wheeler. "The Social Welfare Consequences of General Revenue Sharing." *Public Welfare,* Summer 1972, 5.

10. Wilbur Cohen. "The New Federalism: Theory, Practice, Problems." *National Journal,* special report, March 1973, 14.

11. Thomas J. Anton, Patrick Larkey, Toni Linton, Joel Epstein, John Fox, Nancy Townsend, and Claudia Zawacki. *Understanding the Fiscal Impact of General Revenue Sharing.* Ann Arbor, Mich.: Institute of Public Policy Studies, June 30, 1975, pp. 1–2.

12. Advisory Commission on Intergovernmental Relations, "Final Report of the Advisory Commission on Intergovernmental Relations." Washington, D.C.: U.S. Government Printing Office, 1955, p. 2.

13. Walter Heller. *New Dimensions of Political Economy.* Cambridge, Mass.: Harvard University Press, 1966, pp. 144–147.

14. Martha Derthick. *The Influence of Federal Grants: Public Assistance in Massachusetts.* Cambridge: Harvard University Press, 1972, p. 224.

15. David A. Caputo and Richard L. Cole. *Urban Politics and Decentralization: The Case of General Revenue Sharing.* Lexington, Ky.: D.C. Heath, 1974, pp. 26–27.

16. Ibid., pp. 22–23.

17. Subcommittee on the Planning Process and Urban Development of the Department of Housing and Urban Development, *Revenue Sharing and the Planning Process: Shifting the Locus of Responsibility for Domestic Problem Solving.* Washington, D.C.: National Academy of Sciences, 1974, pp. 41–42.

18. Republican Coordinating Committee, *Financing the Future of Federalism: The Case for Revenue Sharing.* Washington, D.C.: Task Force on the Functions of Federal, State and Local Government, March 1968.

19. Caputo and Cole, p. 29.

20. Ibid., pp. 29–30.

21. Peter F. Drucker. *Age of Discontinuity.* New York: Harper and Row, 1968.

22. Daniel Moynihan. *Maximum Feasible Misunderstanding.* Glencoe, Ill.: Free Press, 1969.

23. James L. Sundquist, with the collaboration of David W. Davis. *Making Federalism Work: A Study of Program Coordination at the Community Level.* Washington, D.C.: The Brookings Institution, 1969, p. 1.

24. Edward Banfield. *The Unheavenly City.* New York: Little, Brown, 1970.

25. Richard Goodwin. "The Shape of American Politics." *Commentary,* June 1967, 36.

26. Richard P. Nathan, Allen D. Manuel, and Susannah E. Calkins. *Monitoring Revenue Sharing.* Washington, D.C.: The Brookings Institution, 1975, pp. 14–18.

27. Wallace Oates. "Introduction." In Robert P. Inman, et al., *Financing the New Federalism,* pp. 1–12.

28. State of Wisconsin, Department of Local Affairs and Development, "Memorandum" (Madison 1974), p. 8.

29. Richard P. Nathan. "Statement on Revenue Sharing," Senate Subcommittee on Intergovernmental Relations, June 5, 1974.

30. State of Wisconsin, Department of Local Affairs and Development, p. 5.

31. Comptroller General of the United States. "Case Studies of Revenue Sharing in 26 Local Governments," *Report to the Subcommittee on Intergovernmental Relations, Committee on Government Operations, U.S. Senate.* Washington, D.C.: Government Printing Office, July 21, 1975, p. 3.

32. Nathan et al., p. 133.

33. Ibid., p. 133.

34. Comptroller General of the United States. "Revenue Sharing: Its Use by and Impact on Local Governments," *Report to the Congress.* Washington, D.C.: Government Printing Office, April 25, 1974.

35. Ibid., pp. 14–15.

36. Mayor Moon Landrieu. "Statement at the Revenue Sharing Oversight Hearings before the Senate Government Operations Subcommittee on Intergovernmental Relations." Washington, June 11, 1974, p. 8.

37. Dry-Lands Research Institute. "The Effects of General Revenue Sharing on Ninety-Seven Cities in Southern California," University of California, Riverside, 1975, pp. 6–7.

38. Nathan et al., p. 133.

39. David A. Caputo and Richard L. Cole. "Initial Decisions in General Revenue Sharing." *Municipal Yearbook,* Washington, D.C.: International City Management Association, 1974, pp. 95–102.

40. Comptroller General of the United States. "Revenue Sharing: Its Use by and Impact on Local Governments," pp. 14–15.

41. Comptroller General of the United States. "Case Studies of Revenue Sharing in 26 Local Governments," p. 8.

42. Department of the Treasury. Office of Revenue Sharing, *General Revenue Sharing: Reported Uses 1973–1974.* Washington, D.C.: U.S. Printing Office, 1975, pp. 37–39.

43. Caputo and Cole. *Urban Politics and Decentralization,* pp. 67–90.

44. Anton et al., p. 10.

45. Ibid., pp. 113–115.

Chapter 6

SUMMARY FOR PART I

From a minimal federal presence under Early Federalism, there has been dramatic growth of centralized power and control. With the process of industrialization and urbanization, it became clear that weak federal government and the unchecked free market could not provide the basic security demanded by the growing middle class. In the 1900s, the Progressives and others created the groundwork for much of the reform activity that was to reach a climax in the social welfare legislation of the 1930s. It became clear that a national presence was needed in the economy and that the social problems created by industrialization and urbanization under a free market system could not be solved by the private sector, the localities, or the states alone.

From 13 colonies, the United States grew into a large, differentiated, specialized, urbanized, interdependent country. Mass communications and the breakup of small, mutual aid-type communities, along with rising expectations, have increased the need for government intervention at the regional and national level. No longer can a local community be solely and totally responsible for problems such as poverty, old age, and mental illness. National direction becomes essential. However, as national needs and financing have become established, there has been a centralization of power in Washington.

And, as problems were found to be less amenable to immediate governmental solution, there was a reaction to federal control. Beginning with the Creative Federalism of John Kennedy and Lyndon Johnson and strenghtened by the New Federalism of Richard Nixon and Gerald Ford, a new trend away from increasing federal control has emerged.

In determining the relationship between the federal government and the states and localities, the founding fathers had three broad alternatives. At one extreme was the unitary form of government, with all power concentrated at the national level. At the other extreme was the model of confederation, with a weak national government and strong states. The model agreed on for America was called federalism. Since it entails the sharing of power and responsibilities between the three levels of government, federalism is in between the extreme of the unitary form and confederation.

Although American federalism is in between two extremes, at different times in our history, it has tended toward one direction or the other. There have been four major periods of American federalism. Among other factors, they are distinguished by the relative distribution of power they confer to the various levels of government. They also have had differential consequences for social welfare policy.

Under Early Federalism, the states and the federal government were seen as equal partners. Supreme Court decisions interpreted the U.S. Constitution strictly. All powers that were not specifically identified as federal powers reverted to the states. Some have called this a period of Dual Federalism, with state and federal powers analogous to two parallel streams. In general, it was felt that the least government was the best government. Social welfare services were provided predominantly by local and state government and private charities.

The conditional grant-in-aid was developed during Early Federalism. It was a way for the federal government to induce the states to undertake programs that were deemed in the national interest. Under the conditional grant-in-aid, the federal government could not impose a program on a state. States had to apply for land or money. Initially, the grant-in-aid was provided without conditions. However, the federal government gradually developed the goals and means for each conditional grant-in-aid. Although it developed during Early Federalism, the conditional grant-in-aid was not used extensively until the next period, Cooperative Federalism, and is still used today. Because it gives the federal government control over both goals and means, it is the funding device that has the most potential to centralize power at the federal level.

Cooperative Federalism emerged as the country grew in size and complexity and problems became national in scope. The Civil War confirmed that states did not have unlimited power. The Great Depression created a national crisis that provided the opportunity for a federal response. In contrast to Early Federalism, Cooperative Federalism involves more intermingling of federal and state governmental functions. Both units of government work together, sharing power and functions. If Early Federalism is analogous to a two-layer cake, with one layer representing the national government and the other layer representing the state government, Cooperative Federalism is analogous to a marble cake, with a mixing up of the two levels of government. During Cooperative Federalism, the federal government used the conditional grant-in-aid extensively. To some extent, the term Cooperative Federalism is misleading, since this was a period when the federal government increased its power significantly. Especially during the Great Depression and the two World Wars, the federal government seemed to be the more powerful of the two levels of government.

During Cooperative Federalism, the federal government provided extensive social welfare services. A series of Supreme Court decisions reflected changing beliefs about the role of government. The general welfare clause in the U.S. Constitution was seen as permitting the federal government to support broad social welfare services, and Social Security was enacted in 1935. Since then, federal involvement in the broad area of social welfare has grown significantly and dramatically, until spending for human services now comprises over half of the federal budget.

The increase in federal power and the movement toward a unitary form of government had in them the seeds of an opposite trend. With the large expansion of the number and types of conditional grants-in-aid came a degree of inefficiency and confusion. Policymakers reacted with calls for simplification and greater efficiency through the strengthening of local and state governments. The Creative Federalism of John Kennedy and Lyndon Johnson can be seen as a beginning of the trend to transfer some power and authority from the federal government to the states and the cities. For the first time in any major way, the cities were recognized as a part of the federal system, and grants were provided directly to them. Decentralization went a step further. There was a major effort to involve citizens in the policy process. Provisions for resident participation, to the maximum feasible extent, were found in much of the legislation of the time. Finally, coordination of the diverse conditional grant-in-aid program was emphasized under Creative Federalism. Most federal agencies, such as the Department of Health, Education and Welfare, the Department of Labor, and the Department of Agriculture, established coordinating and planning bodies on the community level.

A new funding mechanism, the block grant, was used to achieve these goals. The block grant is similar to the conditional grant-in-aid in all but one respect. Under the block grant, states and localities have the freedom to determine the means, or particular programs, that will be used to implement federal goals. The block grant thus gives more power and decision making authority to the states and localities than the conditional grant-in-aid.

In social welfare, the period of Creative Federalism saw an important increase in federal social welfare legislation. In a series of acts, reminiscent of the early days of Franklin D. Roosevelt, Congress passed laws in areas such as civil rights, employment and training, physical and mental health, and poverty. Many of these bills, including the Poverty Program and Model Cities, were directed to helping the urban poor. The Poverty Program was a combination of conditional grants-in-aid and block grants. A section of the Poverty Program was the Community Action Program. Like Model Cities, it was a block grant. Although it had the same goal as Model Cities, the Community Action Program had a different strategy for delivering services and was based on different assumptions about social change. Where the Community Action Program was created outside of City Hall, Model Cities was placed under the control of the mayor. The Community Action Program relied primarily on citizen pressure and the development of interest groups composed of low-income residents to achieve some of its goals. Model Cities, on the other hand, used a more centralized, social planning approach to change.

The New Federalism of Richard Nixon can be seen as a continuation of the decentralization trend started under Creative Federalism. It was also an effort to reduce some of the social welfare programs of the 1960s. The key feature of the New Federalism was a program called General Revenue Sharing, which sent federally collected monies back to the states, counties, and municipalities with almost no federal control. This was a radically different type of funding mechanism. Table 6–1 compares the power of the various levels of government and the three types of federal funding mechanisms.

Table 6–2 combines the discussion of the different types of federalism and the different types of federal grants.

Today, all types of federal programs are available to states and localities. All governmental units automatically receive General Revenue Sharing funds. All have the option to participate, if they wish, in various types of block grants and conditional grants-in-aid.

Table 6-1   Power of Different Levels of Government and
Type of Federal Grant

High federal power Low state and local power	Medium federal power Medium state and local power	Low federal power High state and local power
Conditional grant-in-aid	Block grant	General revenue sharing

Table 6-2   Type of Federalism, Type of Federal Grant,
and Power of Different Levels of Government

	Type of federalism			
	Early federalism (1785)[a]	Cooperative federalism (1935)[a]	Creative federalism (1964)[a]	New federalism (1972)[a]
Type of grant	Conditional grant-in-aid ———————————————————————→ Block ————————→ grant			General revenue sharing
Federal government specifies	Goals Means		Goals	None
State and/or local government specifies	None		Means	Goals Means
State and/or local initiative in applying for grant	State initiative		State and/or local initiative	Automatic

[a]Dates are approximations.

Since they have developed over the longest period of time, grant-in-aid programs are most numerous. However, the current trend is to consolidate many of the grant-in-aid programs into block grants, thus achieving some federal purpose and some state and local control.

To some extent, the debate about the appropriate role of various levels of government, and especially the role of the federal government in social welfare, has developed along philosophical and ideological lines. Individualists have deemphasized the role of all government. They have felt that in the economy, the market should work relatively unencumbered. In the political area, individualists have favored citizen and interest group participation in the determination of policy. When government programs are needed, individualists have supported the government closest to the people as most appropriate. In other words, they prefer local to state government and state government to federal government. Further, individualists favor the least amount of government control. They prefer general revenue sharing to block grants and block grants to conditional grants-in-aid. Finally, individualists deemphasize the effects of environment, family upbringing, and heredity in explaining human behavior.

Humanitarians, on the other hand, have been quicker to support government intervention in the economy. Since they feel that individual behavior is due to a complex interaction of social and psychological conditions, including class, race, family composition, neighborhood, and institutional arrangements, they have been more ready to change situations and institutions that affect people adversely. In the areas of social welfare policy, humanitarians give more support to state and federal control. In the area of politics, humanitarians have felt that powerful interest groups at the local level generally have excluded the poor and others who need help, and that greater control by the federal government will benefit these minorities. From one perspective, the history of federalism, in the area of social welfare, at least, is the history of the debate between those with an individualistic orientation and those with a humanitarian orientation.

Considering the current decline in acceptance of the humanitarians, it is important for those concerned with social welfare policy to place increased attention on the municipal level of decision making. Part II describes a general model of decision making on the municipal level. It then presents an empirical study that identifies community factors that help to explain allocations for social services for the poor at the municipal level under different types of federalism.

Part II

AN EMPIRICAL ANALYSIS OF COMMUNITY DECISION MAKING FOR SOCIAL WELFARE

Chapter 7

COMMUNITY DECISION MAKING

INTRODUCTION

The New Federalism focuses on local community decision making. To the extent that federal power is diminished, it is important to understand how policy decisions are made on the community level. What are the community variables that explain local decision making? Who are the most important actors? This chapter will answer these and other related questions. The first part of the chapter describes the background of community power and decision making studies and contains a model of fundamental variables in community decision making. The second part discusses some of these variables, which will be used in an empirical study of community decision making.

Many terms are used in a specific way. Unless otherwise stated, "community" refers to the legal-geographical entity, such as a city or a suburb, which is the arena for decision making about public policy. For example, Floyd Hunter was referring to Atlanta, Georgia when he wrote his book, *Community Power Structure: A Study of Decision Makers.* [1] "Community Variables" include all the independent variables that could explain allocations for social welfare on the community level. "Neighborhood organizations" refer to locality or neighborhood-based groups that attempt to influence community decision making.

BACKGROUND: PLURALISM AND POWER ELITES

The field of community decision making started formally with the publication of Floyd Hunter's book, *Community Power Structure* in 1953. [2] Hunter asked informants in Atlanta, Georgia to identify powerful individuals. On the basis of these interviews, Hunter concluded that a small number of businessmen and professionals constituted a power elite. He described a pyramidal power structure, in which very few individuals possessed the potential to affect community decision making.

John Walton writes that *Community Power Structure* can be called a classic. Its lasting significance stems partly from Hunter's creation of the term "power structure." This term has been used extensively by social scientists and political activists. Hunter also formulated a new method for studying community power structures, later called the reputational approach. Finally Hunter was the first to apply sociological techniques to the study of the community. Previous studies by sociologists had focused on smaller units, such as the gang, the neighborhood, or the factory. Since *Community Power Structure* was published, more than 500 books and articles have been written on the topic. [3]

After the publication of Hunter's work, case studies of other cities were undertaken. They often used different methods and, in different communities, generally did not find as centralized a power structure as Hunter did.

The most famous of the studies that seemed to contradict

Hunter were Robert A. Dahl's *Who Governs?* and Edward C. Banfield's *Political Influence.* Dahl studied decisions in New Haven, Connecticut, and Banfield studied decision making in Chicago. Using a different method than Hunter, they reconstructed specific decisions in a few community issue areas. Both Dahl and Banfield described pluralistic decision making structures. By pluralistic, they meant that different actors became more involved in decisions in different issue areas, like education or urban renewal. They found also that the actors involved across many issue areas were elected political officials, primarily the mayor.[4]

The differences between the elitists—the followers of Hunter—and the pluralists—the followers of Dahl and Banfield —produced intense debate. Dahl and the pluralists criticized Hunter's method. They suggested that by creating a relatively small panel and asking panel members to identify a few community leaders who had the reputation for being powerful, there was a greater probability of identifying a small power structure. Furthermore, they said Hunter was not studying the exercise of power or influence, but just the potential to use power. To discover who really governs, one must make case studies of individual decisions.[5]

The approaches of the elitists and the pluralists defined alternative conceptions of community power. Followers of Hunter and of Dahl and Banfield sought to extend the initial results by conducting additional case studies of decision making in individual cities. By the mid-1960s, studies of 166 cities had been completed. Efforts to compare them quantitatively, however, suggested the unreliability, or at least the low comparability, of the different case studies.[6]

In the late 1960s comparative studies of two, three, or four communities were undertaken, and a shift in perspective began to emerge.[7] A general continuum ranging from centralization to decentralization was recognized as more accurate empirically than the conceptions of either elitism or pluralism. Socioeconomic characteristics of communities were linked with centralization in a series of propositions amenable to empirical testing.

A conceptual distinction also was made between power as the access to resources and influence as the making of concrete decisions. Thus, power refers to potential, but not necessarily to exerted influence. Influence is conceived of as the making of decisions that cause change. Correspondingly, a power structure (a patterned distribution of power) could be distinguished from a decision making structure (a patterned distribution of influence).[8] The reputational approach of Hunter was thus seen as operationalizing power, while the decisional approach of Dahl and Banfield was an operationalization of influence. Results from the two methods should not have been expected to be identical, since two different phenomena were being studied. This conceptual distinction clarified earlier conflicting results.

After looking at the major studies of community decision making, John Walton has identified several general points of agreement. There is general consensus, for example, that power and influence are distributed differentially in communities among leaders, participants, and the general population. Only a small percentage of a community's citizens actively participate in community decision making. The distribution of power and influence does have an effect on what gets done and what does not get done and on who benefits. Although the power structure and decision making structure variables are not the only variables that determine what gets done and who benefits and are not always the most significant variables, there is agreement in the literature that they must be considered in any study of community decision making.

A second point of general agreement is that through a variety of techniques, leadership structures can be identified reliably and validly. Generally, leaders comprise a small percentage of the total population and often are aligned with or selected from top political and business sectors. Other interests also may be represented. The literature does not necessarily imply elitist or centralized structures.

A third point is that the organizational structures of a city are important in explaining power arrangements and policy outcomes. Public agencies, corporations, voluntary associations, and ethnic, neighborhood, and civil rights organizations all can affect the community decision making process, either individually or in coalitions. Finally the literature points out that democratic participation, such as voting and direct action by interest groups, can have an effect on policy.[9]

A MODEL OF COMMUNITY DECISION MAKING

These conclusions are all very broad. In addition to these general areas of agreement, studies of community decision making have identified a series of variables that could be important in describing and affecting the community decision making process. The old distinction between elitists and pluralists has been seen as too simplistic. Additional factors contribute to the community decision making process.

Fundamental variables important in community decision making are summarized in an input-output flowchart, shown in Figure 7–1.[10] Similar figures appear in several studies.

"Inputs to the community" and "national societal characteristics" act as general constraints on local decision making, mediated by "community characteristics" (demographic, economic, legal-political, organizational, cultural). These, in turn, influence "centralization of power and decision making" and "leadership," with leadership defined in terms of the characteristics of leaders (e.g., businessmen versus politicians). In turn, these variables generate "policy outputs," such as expenditures for social services. Finally, policy outputs feed back on earlier variables to exert "policy impacts," or changes resulting from the policy outputs (such as decreased social problems).

Several large-scale comparative studies were undertaken in the late 1960s in an effort to estimate precise empirical relationships among variables of the sort depicted in Figure 7–1. Per-

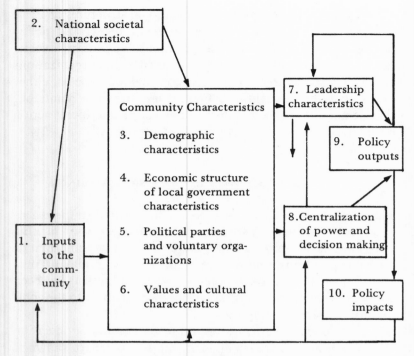

Figure 7–1   Fundamental Variables in Community Decision
Making.

haps the most ambitious efforts were related to the Permanent
Community Sample of the National Opinion Research Center
at the University of Chicago. The first study was of 51 communities, ranging from 50,000 to 750,000 in population directed by
Terry N. Clark of the University of Chicago.[11] The 51-com-
munity study data were used in the research reported in this
book.

Research Methods For Studying Community Power and Influence

Three basic methods have been used for measuring power and
influence: the positional method, the reputational method, and

the decisional method. The positional method begins by establishing a list of occupants of important positions in the community, such as the mayor, the head of the largest bank, and the editor of the major newspaper. Generally, some kind of information is then collected about these leaders, such as social background data from published sources. Problems with this approach include difficulty in developing valid criteria for the selection of important positions and then inferring the amount of influence wielded.

For the reputational approach, first used by Floyd Hunter, a panel of community informants is created. This panel is asked to identify leaders as defined by some criterion. For example, the panel might be asked to identify "persons who are important in getting things done in this town." Results then may be summarized, as in the positional method. A disadvantage of the reputational method is that it tends to assume a pyramidal structure, at least in the sense that it does not explicitly distinguish separate issue areas or levels of involvement in decisions. A variation of this approch is the issue-specific reputational approach, in which informants are asked to rank or score individual community actors in terms of their power in specific issue areas. As in the 51 community study, informants may be asked, "If someone wanted to initiate an urban renewal program in this community, how important would the support of the following actors be?" The informant then scores a list of actors on a scale from high to low.

The method thus does not assume generality of power, but makes possible the empirical analysis of leadership across issue areas. Both the reputational method and the issue-specific reputational method are used to operationalize power instead of influence because of their focus on potential and not exercised influence.

Finally, there is the decisional method initially used by Dahl and by Banfield. The decisional method involves tracing the history of a specific decision or decisions through its basic stages. For example, the investigator studies who initiated an action, who supported this action, who opposed it, who mediated between the conflicting groups, and who prevailed. By studying several community decisions, it is possible to determine whether a few actors are influential in all areas or if many different actors participate in the decision-making structure. Finally, the decisional method helps to identify leaders according to their degree of involvement. But the approach does not identify indirect influence or deal with the problem of "nondecisions." Also, it is often impractical to study each community decision as carefully as this approach requires.

COMMUNITY VARIABLES

Community variables shown in Figure 7–1, Fundamental Variables in Community Decision Making were used in the study and and are described in detail below.

Inputs to the Community

Extra local policies and programs all affect the community. Their form—conditional grant-in-aid, block grant, or general revenue sharing—is important. In recent years there has been a recognition that inputs to the community, especially from the state and federal governments have changed the structure of the community.

Roland Warren writes in the *Community in America* [12] that communities are facing the loss of their autonomy and a lack of identification of residents with the community. These changes result primarily from the increase and type of community inputs. Warren feels that the old horizontal pattern of relationships among community institutions is being replaced by vertical relationships between community institutions and extra-local community units. This change weakens the community as an integrated social system. Warren recommended a community development strategy aimed at restoring the cohesion of the community.[13] The loss of power and control by the local community has been shown in the historical section. The empirical section will study community decision making under different inputs to the community with different degrees of extra-local control.

Demographic and Economic Variables

Demographic variables traditionally have been employed to explain various aspects of community functioning. For example Michael Aiken and Robert Alford concluded that city size and age were the two most important factors in determining a city's score on their measure of innovation.[14] However, the dependent variables included decisions cities made about programs starting in 1933, 1949, and 1964, while the independent variables were based primarily on material from the 1960 Census. Finally, Aiken and Alford use a measure which emphasized the cumulative nature of program expenditures. Their measure of innovation is sensitive to when a city initiates a program, the cumulative size of the program, and the fact that a city participates in a program. This type of measure would seem to favor older and larger cities when programs starting in 1933 and 1949 are considered.[15]

Kristen Grønbjerg studied the effect of stratification and mass society variables on State AFDC rolls. She identified median level of education, class, and population increase, among others, as important demographic factors.[16]

Terry Clark has suggested that richer communities demand and are willing to pay for a higher level of services than poorer communities. Therefore, the wealth of a city affects community policy.[17]

While there does not seem to be a consensus about which demographic and economic factors are most important, it is clear that they are significant variables which must be considered in any study of community decision making.

Structure of Local Government

Political scientists have been interested in the consequences of the reform movement in city government on policy outputs. When policy outputs are considered, how do cities with a strong mayor differ from those with a council-manager type of government? Does the power of the mayor influence policy outputs? In the 51-community study, there was a slight tendency for cities with reform characteristics to spend more, in general, than those with nonreform characteristics. This variable, therefore, must be considered in any study of community decision making.

Political Parties and Voluntary Associational Activity

There has been strong support for the thesis that participation can influence policy at the community level.[18] In *Participation in America,* Sidney Verba and Norman Nie demonstrate that participation can have an effect on policy output. Verba and Nie's study, based on a national survey conducted in 1967 by the National Opinion Research Corporation, confirms previous conclusions that participation in America is strongly dependent on the socioeconomic model. In other words, the higher the socioeconomic status of an individual, the higher the level of participation. Verba and Nie also distinguish between seven different types of participation, including voting behavior and communal activities, that benefit the common good.[19]

Participation in political and voluntary associational activity should be considered in explaining decision making on the community level. It is generally assumed that policy outputs increase directly with participation, but the converse also could be true. In cities with high participation rates in specific policy areas, conflict between groups might stall governmental action and lower outputs.

Values

The extent to which opinions and values influence policy is a topic of current concern. Verba and Nie have shown that upper-class persons, who participate and are effective to a greater degree than middle- and lower-class persons, are more conservative than the general population. On the issues of integration, public welfare, and governmental involvement in social welfare, upper-class persons consistently are unrepresentative and more conservative than the population in general.[20]

A recent approach to studying citizen choices asks respondents to rank their preferences for various governmental services and indicate for what services they would be willing to pay more tax.[21] Values, therefore, could differ from community to community and play a significant role in policy determinations.

Leadership

A central concern in urban areas is who exerts power and influence. The earliest case studies showed businessmen to be most central. At other times, the mayor and political actors were seen as most important. Some studies showed businessmen and politicians collaborating in differing degrees with other community actors. Not surprisingly, the comparative studies revealed similar diversity. But the diversity of the comparative studies is nevertheless structured. There are consistent results that have recurred over enough cities to make them important enough to remember.

Studies by Clark, by Laumann, Verbrugge, and Pappi, by Morlock, and by Rossi, Berk, and Eidson[22] have focused on leadership. All four identify two patterns of city leadership: one centered around the mayor and his or her office, and a second centered on business leaders, civic groups, and newspapers. The relative mixture, however, varies considerably across cities. Although there are a few cities where the mayor and his or her office are central actors, and others where business actors are more central, most cities have diverse coalitions involving these and other actors in varying mixes. Nevertheless, in most cities the three key actors remain the mayor, leading businessmen, and the newspaper.

The comparative studies distinguish two general tendencies that differentiate cities. One tendency is more associated with business and newspaper leadership. Civic elite groups and the chamber of commerce also are likely to be important actors in these business-oriented cities. Business-oriented cities tend to be found more often in the West, in cities that have smaller populations, city managers, nonpartisanship at large elections, and more affluent citizens who tend to vote Republican. By contrast, political actors, especially the mayor, political parties, and sometimes labor-union leaders and heads of government agencies, tend to be more important in the Midwest and the East, in cities with larger populations, more industry, mayor-council government, partisan and ward-based elections, middle-income residents, Roman Catholics, and immigrants from central and southern Europe. In most instances, however, such generalizations are clearer and more consistent for the power structure than for the decision-making structure.[23]

Centralization

Centralization often is conceptualized and measured in terms of two dimensions: participation and overlap. The larger the number of participants and the less their overlap across issue areas, the less centralized the community's power structure or decision making structure. Cities are likely to have more centralized power and decision making structures if they:

—Are small in population.

—Are economically nondiversified (there are few employers and types of employment).

—Do not have competitive political parties or many voluntary associations.

—Have nonpartisan elections.

—Have at-large electoral constituencies.

Further, the degree of centralization is likely to vary within the same community, depending on the issue. For example, it would be possible to have a centralized decision making structure in social welfare in a generally decentralized city.

Recent studies have deemphasized the importance of centralization in comparison with other variables in community decision making studies.[24]

Policy Outputs

Policy outputs are the result of collective and mainly governmental decision making. They traditionally have been measured by fiscal indicators.[25] For example, the amount of money that a community spends on social services is a fiscal indicator.

At least two factors may be important when considering the policy output of centralized and decentralized decision making structures. The first factor is whether the policy is a more public or a more separable good; the second is the degree of fragility of the policy. A pure public good is produced by government and consumed by all citizens. A public good may be supplied jointly to several individuals without the increased consumption of one individual affecting the availability of the good for other individuals. An example is fluoridation. If individual A consumes fluoridated water, so does individual B. And A's consumption level does not decrease B's. In contrast, separable goods may be allocated to specific subpopulations. They thus may benefit one group in the population while taking resources from others.

Fragile decisions tend to be more controversial decisions. They deal with policies and programs that are new to a community, with relatively unpopular policies and policies that benefit less powerful members of the communities.

Conceptually, a continuum can be developed for public goods and fragile decisions. Every policy output could be located somewhere on each continuum. Many programs of interest to social workers that benefit distinct sections of the population, such as the poor and emotionally ill, tend to be separable and fragile. As we move toward more universal programs and policies (e.g., social services for all as a basic right), we move toward the province of public goods.

Some studies have attempted to relate the degree of centralization of a decision making structure to the issues of public and separable goods and fragility. In general, according to Larry Lyon, the results have not been conclusive.[26] Social services for the poor, the main concern of this book, can be classified as a separable good and as services that involve a fragile or controversial decision. However, community factors that explain separable and fragile decisions may not be important in explaining other types of decisions.

CONCLUSION

This chapter has reviewed the historical, conceptual, and empirical development of the study of community decision making. Based on past research, the variables of input to the community, demographic characteristics, economic characteristics, structure of local government, political parties and voluntary organizations, values and cultural characteristics, leadership characteristics, and centralization are seen to contribute to policy outputs at the local level.

The next chapter will describe a study design whose purpose is to determine if any of these variables together or separately can explain policy output for social welfare programs that benefit low-income persons. The programs selected, the Poverty Program, the Community Action Program, the Model Cities Program, and Social Services under General Revenue Sharing, represent conditional grants-in-aid, block grants, and General Revenue Sharing.

NOTES

1. Floyd Hunter. *Community Power Structure: A Study of Decision-Makers.* Chapel Hill, N.C.: University of North Carolina Press, 1953.

2. Ibid.

3. John Walton. "The Bearing of Social Science Research on Public Issues: Floyd Hunter and the Study of Power." In John Walton and Donald E. Carns. *Cities in Change: Studies on the Urban Social Condition,* second ed., Boston: Allyn and Bacon, 1977, pp. 263–72.

4. Edward C. Banfield. *Political Influence.* New York: Free Press, 1960; Robert A. Dahl. *Who Governs? Democracy Power in an American City,* New Haven, Conn.: Yale University Press, 1961.

5. Walton, Ibid.

6. Terry N. Clark. *Community Power and Policy Outputs: A Review of Urban Research.* Beverly Hills, Calif.: Sage Publications, 1973.

7. Robert Agger, Daniel Goldrich, and Bert Swanson. *The Rulers and the Ruled: Political Power and Impotence in American Communities.* New York: John Wiley, 1964; Michael Aiken and Paul Mott, eds. *The Structure of Community Power.* New York: Random House, 1970; Terry N. Clark. *Community Structure and Decision-Making: Comparative Analyses.* Scranton, Pa.: Chandler Publishing, 1968; Robert Presthus. *Men at*

the Top: A Study of Community Power. New York: Oxford University Press, 1964.

8. Clark, *Community Structure and Decision-Making,* pp. 46–47.

9. Walton, Ibid.

10. Ibid., p. 18; Robert L. Crain, Elihu Katz, and Donald B. Rosenthal. *The Politics of Community Conflict: The Fluoridation Decision.* Indianapolis: Bobbs-Merrill, 1967; Brian T. Downes, ed. *Cities and Suburbs: Selected Readings in Local Politics and Public Policy.* Belmont, Calif.: Wadsworth Publishing, 1971.

11. Terry N. Clark. "Community Structure, Decision-Making, Budget Expenditures, and Urban Renewal in 51 American Communities." *American Sociological Review, 33,* August 1968, 576–593.

12. Roland Warren. *The Community in America,* second ed., Chicago: Rand McNally, 1972.

13. Ibid.

14. Michael Aiken and Robert Alford. "Community Structure and Innovation," in Clark, ed., *Comparative Community Politics,* 1974.

15. Ibid.

16. Kristen A. Grønbjerg. "Mass Society and the Extension of Welfare 1960–1970." Ph.D. Thesis, Department of Sociology, University of Chicago, June 1974.

17. Terry N. Clark. "Money and the Cities," mimeographed, 51 pages.

18. Robert S. Magill. "Joining Formal Voluntary Associations and Social Action Among the Poor." *The Journal of Voluntary Action Research,* October 1973, 224-229.

19. Sidney Verba and Norman H. Nie. *Participation in America.* New York: Harper and Row, 1972.

20. Ibid.

21. Terry N. Clark. "Can You Cut a Budget Pie?" *Policy and Politics, 3,* December 1974, 3–32.

22. Terry N. Clark. "Leadership in American Cities: Resources, Interchanges and the Press." Unpublished manuscript, Chicago, June 1973; Edward O. Laumann, Lois M. Verbrugge, and Franz U. Pappi. "A Causal Modeling Approach to the Study of a Community Elite's Influence Structure." *American Sociological Review, 39,* April 1974, 162–174; Laura A. Morlock. "Business Interests, Countervailing Groups and the

Balance of Influence in 91 Cities." In *The Search for Community Power,* second ed., Willis D. Hawley and Frederick M. Wirt, eds., Englewood Cliffs, N.J.: Prentice-Hall, 1974; Peter H. Rossi, Richard A. Berk and Bettye K. Eidson. *The Roots of Urban Discontent.* New York: Wiley-Interscience, 1974.

23. Clark, "Leadership in American Cities."

24. Larry Lyon. "Community Power and Policy Outputs: A Question of Relevance." In Roland Warren, ed. *New Perspectives on the American Community: A Book of Readings,* third ed., Chicago: Rand McNally, 1977, pp. 418–434.

25. Clark, *Community Power and Policy Outputs,* p. 63.

26. Lyon, Ibid.

Chapter 8

THE STUDY

INTRODUCTION

The goal of Part II is to identify factors that can help explain variations in the size of grants for social welfare programs for the poor at the municipal level. The independent variables were chosen from the input-output model of community decision making described in the previous chapter. Specific measures that were used in the study are described in this chapter. The dependent variables, the size of the grants for social welfare programs for the poor, are representative of different approaches to federalism. The Poverty Program as a whole represents the conditional grant-in-aid program characteristic of Early and Cooperative Federalism. The Community Action Program and Model Cities are block grants typical of Creative Federalism. Allocations for social services for the poor and aged under General Revenue Sharing are characteristic of New Federalism. Table 8–1 shows the overall design for the study.

This chapter describes the sample, the statistical techniques, and the specific independent and dependent measures

Table 8-1   Community Variables and Grants for
Social Welfare Programs Under Different Approaches to Federalism

Independent variables	Dependent variables		
	Early and Cooperative Federalism	Creative Federalism	New Federalism
	Conditional grant-in-aid	Block grant	General Revenue Sharing
	Poverty Program	Community Action Program and Model Cities	Allocations for poor and aged under General Revenue Sharing
Demographic variables			
Political and voluntary organizations			
Values			
Structure of municipal government			
Leadership			
Centralization			

used. The next chapter presents the analysis of the data. The
last chapter contains the summary and conclusion.

THE SAMPLE

The communities chosen for the study are from the Permanent
Community Sample. The Permanent Community Sample is a
national sample of American municipalities. It is maintained by
the National Opinion Research Center (NORC) of the University of Chicago. The sample constitutes a representative sample
of the places of residence of the American population (not of
municipalities, per se) and was used in the 51-community study
directed by Terry N. Clark.[1]

Since not all of the municipalities contained in the larger sample participated in all of the programs included in this study, a subsample of the Permanent Community Sample was chosen. Based on the 1960 U.S. Census of the Population, municipalities were selected if they had a population of more than 85,000 persons and less than 310,000 persons. The mean of the subsample was 197,500. The population mean of the total sample was 250,786. The sample used in this study included 22 municipalities. Of these, 18 were central cities of a standard metropolitan statistical area and four were suburbs. The municipalities were well distributed throughout the country. Five were located in the Northeast, six were located in the Midwest, four were located in the South, and seven were located in the West.

Demographic data were collected from the *County and City Data Book,* the *U.S. Census,* the *Compendium of Municipal Finances,* and the *Municipal Yearbook.* In addition, interviews were conducted by the NORC professional field staff in 1967. There were 11 strategically placed persons in each community who were identified as knowledgeable informants. These included the mayor, the chairman of the Democratic and Republican parties, the president of the largest bank, the editor of the newspaper with the largest circulation, the president of the chamber of commerce, the president of the bar association, the head of the largest union, the health commissioner, the urban renewal director, and the director of the last major hospital fund drive. Interview schedules concentrated on both institutional realms of the informants and general community issues.[2]

STATISTICAL METHODS

The two major statistical methods employed in this study are Pearson Product-Moment Correlation Coefficients and Multiple Regression Analysis. The Pearson Product-Moment Correlation Coefficient "... provides a single number which summarizes the relationship between two variables. These correlation coefficients indicate the degree to which variation (or change) in one variable is related to variation (or change) in another. A correlation coefficient not only summarizes the strength of association between a pair of variables, but also provides an easy means for comparing the strength of the relationship between one pair of variables and a different pair."[3]

The Pearson Product-Moment Correlation Coefficient is symbolized by r. It measures a linear relationship and varies between $+1.0$ and -1.0. A positive sign identifies a direct relationship, and a negative sign identifies an inverse relationship between the variables. The value of 0 denotes the absence of a linear relationship between the variables.[4]

The significance of the correlation coefficients—the probability that the observed relationship between the variables depart from zero by chance alone—is also reported. Three levels of significance are used: $* = p\ .05$; $** = p\ .01$; and $*** = p\ .001$. With a significance level of .05, the probability is that the relationship between the variables is not due to chance in 95 percent of samples. Similarly, a significance level of .01 indicates that the observed relationship between the sample variables occurs by chance in a population where there is really no relationship only 1 percent of the time.[5]

"*Multiple regression* is a method of analyzing the collective and separate contributions of two or more independent variables, x_i, to the variation of a dependent variable, Y."[6] Multiple Regression Analysis is a statistical method that can be used to help "explain" the variance of a dependent variable. "It does this, in part, by estimating the contributions to this variance of two or more independent variables."[7]

When the coefficient of correlation is squared, it is called the coefficient of determination and expresses the proportion of variance of Y "determined" by X, or X's, the independent variable(s). R Squared varies between 0 and $+1.0$, indicating the proportion of the dependent variable's variance accounted for by the independent variable(s). For example, an R Square of .82 means that all of the independent variables (Xs) taken together explain 82 percent of the variation in Y, the dependent variable.[8]

Adjusted R Square adjusts the R Square statistic for the number of independent variables and the number of cases. It is a more conservative estimate of the percent of variance explained than R Square, especially when there is a small sample size. The formula used is

$$\text{Adjusted } R^2 = R^2 - \frac{k-1}{n-k}\ (1 - R^2)$$

where k is the number of independent variables in the regression equation, n is the number of cases, and R^2 to the right of the equal sign is the unadjusted R^2.[9]

In order to determine the influence of each of the independent variables on the dependent variable, with the remaining independent variables in the equation held constant, Beta coefficients are used. Like r and R Square, they are standardized, so they are not influenced by the size of units employed in the variables (e.g., pennies or dollars). "Each coefficient . . . represents the amount of change in Y that can be associated with a given change in one of the X's with the remaining independent variables held fixed. . . . (Betas) could be used to give a measure of the direct effects of each of the independent variables in determining variation in Y."[10] "The beta weights . . . indicate *how much change* in the dependent variable is produced by a standardized change in one of the independent variables when the others are controlled."[11]

According to Fred Kerlinger and Elazar Pedhazur, "regression coefficients are perhaps the nearest that scientists get to causal indices." ". . . other things being equal, the larger a regression weight the greater is its variable's contribution to the dependent variable."[12]

Finally, all but one of the dependent variables in this study were skewed and so have been transformed by the application of log 10. Edward R. Tufte, in *Data Analysis for Politics and Policy,* explained the use of log transformations in multiple regression analysis as follows.

"The logarithmic transformation serves several purposes:
1. The resulting regression coefficients sometimes have more useful theoretical interpretation compared to a regression based on unlogged variables.
2. Badly skewed distributions . . . are transformed by taking the logarithm of the measurements so that the clustered values are spread out and the large values pulled in more toward the middle of the distribution.
3. Some of the assumptions underlying the regression model and the associated significance tests are better met when the logarithm of the measured variables is taken."[13]

INDEPENDENT VARIABLES

The study employs an *ex post facto* research design. The independent variables are measures of community factors that explain variation in the dependent variables, the amounts of the grants received by municipalities for various social welfare programs.

The independent variable measures are listed in Appendix A. They are organized in terms of whether they are demographic and economic variables, legal and political variables, political parties and voluntary associational activity, values and cultural characteristics, leadership, and centralization. In some cases, a measure could be placed in more than one category. For example, the decisional influence of the Republican party leaders and officials measure, while listed under political parties and voluntary associational activity, could also be considered under the category of leadership. These variables are referred to as "community variables" in the tables in the chapter on data analysis.

Independent variables were chosen on the basis of a review of the literature of community decision making. Measures of these variables were selected from over 500 measures contained in the 51-Community study file. Some of these measures were collected in 1967, and others, such as some demographic measures, were added later.

Initially, 127 measures of the six independent variables were selected. These measures were inspected in more detail. Some measures were eliminated because they did not contain enough cases or because they were too skewed or had too high of a kurtosis (the relative peakedness or flatness of the distribution).

Pearson Product-Moment Correlations were run for all of the 500 independent variables and the dependent variables. In a few cases, variables that had not been included in the original independent variable list were included due to their high Pearson Correlation Coefficient.

The literature of community decision making was rereviewed in order to aid in the selection of measures of the independent variable. The most important criteria in the selection of the final independent variable measures were their theoretical importance. In some cases, variables were included, even though their Pearson Product-Moment Correlation Coefficients with the dependent variables were low.

Measures were eliminated from the list on the following basis.

1. There were not enough valid cases or the measure was too skewed or had too high a kurtosis. Some measures that had theoretical importance were eliminated on the basis of these criteria.
2. There was more than one measure of a phenomenon, such as decentralization. Only one measure of decentralization was selected for the final study.
3. Independent variables were strongly intercorrelated with each other.
4. Independent variables were weakly correlated with dependent variables.

The final study includes 18 different measures of the independent variables. Six were measures of political parties and voluntary associational activity, five were measures of leadership variables, four were measures of demographic and economic variables, two were measures of values and cultural characteristics, and one was a measure of centralization. Only six independent variables were used in any regression. The final list of measures of the independent variables and their construction are presented in Appendix A.

The dependent variables were generally measures of the grants made for various programs. Originally, measures were collected of the amount of the City Community Action Program, the City Model Cities Program planning grant, the City Model Cities Program (over a four-year period), allocations for social services under the City Revenue Sharing Program, the County Community Action Program, the County Poverty Program, and the city and county Poverty Program. Measures were also developed for the date cities first received their city Community Action Program grant and their Model Cities planning grant. There was one missing case for one year in the revenue sharing measure. It was assumed that communities that did not receive grants for any of the programs decided not to participate and were coded with a zero. The dependent variable measures and their descriptions are given in Appendix B.

In most cases, the variable names and descriptions do not need further clarification. However, the construction of the leadership and decentralization indexes are more involved. Since it has been shown that the method used can influence results, the construction of these indexes will be discussed.

Power was measured by two types of questions and influence by a third. Power, or the *potential* to affect an actor or a decision, was measured by open-ended and closed-ended issue specific reputational questions. These questions asked about the potential importance of various actors. They differed from Floyd Hunter's approach in that they identified specific issue areas. For example, for the open-ended reputational series, the interviewer asked: "Is there any single person whose opposition would be almost impossible to overcome, or whose support would be essential if someone wanted to . . . ," followed by five different endings: "(run for/ be appointed to) the school board in (city)?; organize a campaign for a municipal bond referendum in (city)?; get the city to undertake an urban renewal project?; . . . essential for a program for the control of air pollution (city)?; run for mayor in (city)?" If the initial response was negative, the informant was asked for the name of the person who "comes closest to this description."[14]

These questions were asked of seven informants in each city. The informants were the president of the chamber of commerce, the chairman of the Democratic party and the chairman of the Republican party, the president of the largest bank, a labor leader, a newspaper editor, and the president of the bar association. Leadership scores for a status, such as mayor, were computed by summing all of the mentions for the status and dividing this by the total mentions for all statuses. With this formula, if one or two statuses received most of the mentions, their scores would be higher than if many statuses received many mentions. The formula for the open-ended reputational items was:

$$L_{sa} = \sum_{i=1}^{7} \frac{s_i}{t_i} \times 100$$

where i refers to the seven informants and a to each of the five issue areas. The leadership score for a status, s (e.g., the newspaper), was computed by summing all mentions for the status s_i and dividing it by that for all statuses, t_i. This was multiplied by 100 to get percentage scores.[15]

For the closed-ended reputational questions, the informant was handed a card with a list of 15 actors. The interviewer stated, "Here is a list of groups and organizations. Please tell me for each whether their support is essential for the success of a candidate for the school board, whether their support is important but not essential, or whether their support is not important." This question was repeated, substituting for the school board "a municipal bond referendum," "an urban renewal project," "a program of air pollution control," and "a candidate for mayor." A score was then computed for each actor, scoring essential as 3, important but not essential as 2, and not important as 1. The preceding formula was used except that $t_i = 51 \times 7 = 357$.[16]

The statuses and organizations on the card handed to each respondent included the Democratic party, Republican party, chamber of commerce, churches, newspapers, bar association, labor unions, ethnic groups, neighborhood groups, heads of local government agencies, city and county employees, industrial leaders, retail merchants, bankers and executives of financial institutions, and other businessmen.

For the decisional scores, informants were asked about four typical issue areas. The issue areas were air pollution, the poverty program, urban renewal, and selecting a mayor. For each area, the informant was essentially asked: Who initiated action on the issue? Who supported this action? Who opposed this action? Who mediated and was involved in negotiating an outcome? Who prevailed? and Which actors were most successful in obtaining their goals? The results for each leadership score were used in the computation formula previously described.[17]

The index of decentralization was created from the decisional series by adding the number of different actors involved in four issue areas. If numerous different actors participated in decisions in different issue areas, the city had a high score on the index of decentralization. If a few actors were perceived to make most decisions on all of the issues, the city was more centralized and received a low score on the index of decentralization.[18]

DEPENDENT VARIABLES

To measure policy outputs, federal-city programs that allow for local decision making and are or can be directed toward low-income persons were selected. They were the Economic Opportunity Act of 1964, the Community Action Section of the Economic Opportunity Act of 1964, the Demonstration and Metropolitan Development Act of 1966, and the State and Local Fiscal Assistance Act of 1972. The Community Action Program, Model Cities, and social services under revenue sharing all allow for some degree of local decision making. They all provide social services for low-income people. They vary in terms of the local agency designated as the major administrative unit. They vary also in terms of the degree to which there is federal control. In the first two, communities had to mobilize themselves and apply for the grants. Under revenue sharing the money was sent automatically from the federal government, and local governments had almost total discretion in determining how it was spent. These programs thus represent different phases of federalism.

The major source for data on the Poverty Program was the U.S. Office of Economic Opportunity's *Poverty Program Information,* as of January 1, 1966, Volumes 1 and 2. This contains a list of all grants awarded as of 1964 and 1965. The grants are listed by community. For each grant, the legal title (e.g., Community Action Program), the amount of the grant, and the date it was given are listed.

Amounts were collected for every kind of grant under the Poverty Program for the first two years for each of the 51 cities. A city that participated in all of the available OEO programs during the first two years could have several grants under sections of the Community Action Program, grants for Volunteers in Service to America (VISTA), the Neighborhood Youth Corp (N.Y.C.), Adult Basic Education, Work Experience Program, Rural Loans, and Head Start. Descriptions of the services provided under each Community Action Program grant also were collected. In data analysis, the total Community Action Program grant was separated from the total amount of the Poverty Program funds that a city received. Data were coded also for the date the city first received its Community Action Grant, and the total amount of the OEO grant.

In some cases, a city and a county were geographically coterminous, or the County Community Action Agency had the city's name in it. In those cases, a new category, separate from the city category, was created. This category contained too few cases and was not used in final data analysis. Finally, in some cases, there was a County Community Action Program, or a City Community Action Program and a County Community Action Program. In those cases, a third category, representing the total county Community Action Program grant (not including the city grant) was coded. Corresponding data for the City-County Poverty Program and the County Poverty Programs were also collected.

Data for the Model Cities Program were taken from the Department of Housing and Urban Development's publication, "Model Cities Grants Approved Through 12/31/72," Washington, D.C., April 4, 1973. The first grant listed for each city was the planning grant and was coded separately. The date that this grant was received was also coded. The total of all of the grants a city received over the course of the program was also coded.

Data for the Revenue Sharing Program were collected from the Actual Use Reports that were published for each city for the first two years of the program. The total amount that a city reported for the first two years in operating/maintenance expenditures and/or capital expenditures for the categories of "Social Services for Aged and Poor" and "Social Development" was included. All grants for all programs were coded in thousands of dollars.

An interval scale was developed and a weight was assigned to the date that communities first received Community Action Program monies and Model Cities planning grants. The weighting procedure was created so that the dates could be ranked in favor of the early receipt of funds. For example, for the City Community Action grants, a list was created of all of the months from November 1964, the date of the first grant, to December 1965, the date of the last grant in the sample. Starting with December 1965 and working backward, increments of 40 were added. Under this formula, a city that received an early grant had a higher score than one that received a later grant. Similar procedures were used to code the date the first grant was received for City/County Community Action Program, the County Community Action Program, and the Model Cities Planning Grant.

The nine dependent variables originally selected as measures of policy output for the programs were:

1. The City Community Action Program date measures the date on which a city received its first Community Action Program Grant.
2. The City Community Action Program Grant is the amount of the city's total Community Action Program Grant for the first two years.
3. The County Community Action Program grant is a similar measure for the county level only.
4. The County Poverty Total includes all monies that only counties received under the Poverty Program.
5. All Poverty Totals include the total amount a city and county received under the Poverty Program.
6. The Model Cities date measures the date a city first received its Model Cities Planning Grant.
7. The Model Cities plan is comparable to the City Community Action Program measure and includes the total amount of the Model Cities Planning Grant.
8. The Model Cities total includes the total amount of money a city received over the life of the Model Cities Program.
9. Revenue Sharing measures the amount of money, during the first two years, that cities allocated for social services, divided by the total amount of their Revenue Sharing Grant.

Table 8-2 presents the Product-Moment Correlations among the dependent variables.

In Table 8-2, it may be seen that the two measures of the City Community Action Program, City Community Action Program date and City Community Action Program were almost perfectly correlated ($r = .996$***). The date on which a city received its Community Action Program Grant was positively related to the amount of the grant. Cities that received early Community Action Program grants also received the largest amount of grants. The relationship was so strong that one variable only, City Community Action Program, was retained for further analysis.

The three Model Cities measures were intercorrelated to almost the same degree. The r for Model Cities date with the Model Cities plan reached .989*** and, with the total amount spent for Model Cities, .990***. The Model Cities plan was also highly correlated with the total amount spent for Model Cities ($r = .995$***). Cities that participated early in the program spent more money for the planning grant and for the total amount of the Model Cities Program. Therefore, the measures of the date a city first received its Model Cities grant and the amount of the total Model Cities grant were eliminated from the study as redundant, retaining the amount of the Model Cities plan as the indicator for this cluster of variables.

Table 8-3 presents the Product-Moment Correlations among the revised list of dependent variables.

The largest correlation coefficient in Table 8-3 is between the city Community Action Program and the Model Cities Program ($r = .587$**). This is consistent with earlier expectations, discussed in the chapter on Creative Federalism. The Community Action Program and Model Cities were a part of Lyndon Johnson's Creative Federalism. Both are block grants to localities, and both were part of the more general policy to reduce poverty and improve urban social, economic, and physical conditions.

Table 8–2 Product-Moment Correlations Among Dependent Variables

	2	3	4	5	6	7	8	9
1. City Community Action Program date	.996***	-.069	.306	.154	.630***	.607***	.624***	-.229
2. City Community Action Program		-.096	.312	.157	.601**	.587**	.606***	-.166
3. County Community Action Program			.437*	.294	.126	.106	.087	-.144
4. County Poverty Total				.584**	.233	.235	.252	.041
5. All Poverty Totals					.141	.149	.151	-.110
6. Model Cities Date						.989***	.990***	-.147
7. Model Cities Plan							.995***	-.036
8. Model Cities Total								-.045
9. Revenue Sharing								—

*** = p .001
** = p .01
* = p .05

Table 8–3 Product-Moment Correlations
Among Revised List of Dependent Variables

	2	3	4	5	6
1. City Community Action Program	−.096	.312	.157	.587**	−.166
2. County Community Action Program		.437*	.294	.106	−.144
3. County Poverty Total			.584**	.235	.041
4. All poverty Totals				.149	−.110
5. Model Cities Plan					−.036
6. Revenue Sharing					—

** = p .01
 * = p .05

However, under General Revenue Sharing, there are no federal requirements about the purpose for which funds can be spent. Table 8–3 shows that, as expected, there are no significant relationships between spending for social services for the poor and aged under General Revenue Sharing and grants under the Community Action Program and Model Cities.

There are two other significant correlated variables in Table 8–3 that need explanation. The County Community Action Program is significantly related to the County Poverty Total ($r = .437*$) because the County Poverty Total includes the county Community Action Total, along with expenditures for other kinds of poverty programs. Similarly, the total amount spent for all programs under the Poverty Program includes the County Poverty Total ($r = .584**$). That is, the County Poverty Total is a part of the total amount spent for all Poverty Programs. The preceding results had been expected. All other intercorrelations are weak and not significant, as expected.

NOTES

1. Terry N. Clark. *Cities Differ—But How and Why?: Inputs to National Urban Policy From Research on Decision-Making in 51 American Municipalities.* Report to Office of Policy Development and Research, U.S. Department of Housing and Urban Development, September, 1975, pp. 7–9.

2. Ibid.

3. Norman H. Nie, C. Hadlai Hull, Jean G. Jenkins, Karin Steinbrenner, Dale H. Bent. *Statistical Package for the Social Sciences.* Second ed. New York: McGraw-Hill, 1975, pp. 276–277.

4. Ibid., p. 279.

5. Ibid.

6. Fred N. Kerlinger and Elazar J. Pedhazur. *Multiple Regression in Behavioral Research.* New York: Holt, Rinehart and Winston, 1973, p. 3.

7. Ibid., p. 4.

8. Ibid., p. 15.

9. Nie et al., p. 358.

10. Hubert M. Blalock. *Social Statistics.* New York: McGraw-Hill, 1972, p. 452–453.

11. Ibid., p. 453.

12. Ibid., p. 446.

13. Edward R. Tufte. *Data Analysis for Politics and Policy.* Englewood Cliffs, N.J.: Prentice-Hall, 1974, p. 108.

14. Clark, "Cities, Differ," pp. 18, 19.

15. Ibid., p. 19.

16. Ibid., p. 21.

17. Ibid., pp. 22, 23.

18. Terry N. Clark. "Community Structure, Decision-Making, Budget Expenditures, and Urban Renewal in 51 American Communities." *American Sociological Review, 33,* August 1968, 576–593.

Chapter 9

DATA ANALYSIS

INTRODUCTION

This chapter presents the analysis of the data. A major purpose is to determine what differences, if any, there may have been among the factors explaining policy output for the Community Action Program, and Model Cities, and social services under General Revenue Sharing. In addition, the County Community Action Program, the County Poverty Program, and all Poverty Programs will be considered. The independent variables were selected from six categories. They are:

1. Demographic characteristics
2. Leadership characteristics
3. Value and cultural characteristics
4. Political and voluntary associational activity
5. Structure of government
6. Decentralization

For the purposes of this chapter, community variables refer to any variable selected from this list.

CITY COMMUNITY ACTION PROGRAM

Table 9-1 presents the results of stepwise multiple regression of certain community variables on the amount of the total city Community Action Grant. The Betas are from the final step, while the R Square and adjusted R Square are from each step and indicate the degree to which each variable entered augments the explained variance.

Table 9-1   Multiple Regression of Community Variables
on the Amount of the Total City Community Action Grant
November 1964 to December 1965[a]

	Beta	R Square	Adjusted R Square
Percent unemployed in 1960	.687***	.224	.224
Percent nonwhite in 1960	.468*	.375	.343
Importance of neighborhood groups	−.509***	.545	.497
City population in 1960	.294	.615	.551
Decisional influence of the mayor	−.296	.678	.603
	Total equation significant at .01		

*** = p .001
 ** = p .01
  * = p .05
[a]City Community Action Grant Variable transformed by Log 10

The total amount of money spent for the Community Action Program is most influenced by demographic type variables. Three of the five variables in the equation are demographic. The most important demographic variable was the percent unemployed in 1960 (Beta = .687***). As expected, there is a direct, strong and significant relationship between percent unemployed and the total City Community Action Grant. Percent nonwhite and the size of the city population each help to explain why some cities spent more than others for the Community Action Program.

A voluntary organization measure and a leadership measure, the importance of neighborhood groups and the decisional influence of the mayor, also help to explain output, although there is an inverse association. These results were unexpected. The inverse relationship between the importance of neighborhood groups and grants for the City Community Action Program can be explained by the high level of conflict in the cities and the neighborhoods when the Community Action Program was created. In many cities, there was antagonism between neighborhood groups as they struggled with each other to get control of the Community Action Program. The result of this conflict between opposing neighborhood groups may have been less of an ability by local communities to organize a Community Action Council and develop a proposal for a Community Action Grant. Therefore, the greater the importance of many neighborhood groups, the greater the conflict and the less the amount of the Community Action Program Grants.

The weakest relationship reported in Table 9–1 is between the decisional influence of the mayor and the amount of the City Community Action Program (Beta $= -.296$). The relationship is inverse, indicating mayor's opposition to the Community Action Program.

Of the city programs studied (Community Action, Model Cities and General Revenue Sharing), the Community Action Program was the only one created outside of city government. This lack of control may be one reason that the mayors opposed community action. The weak relationship may be due to the mayor's resistance to controversial projects or to the mayor's lack of influence.

After studying Chicago in the late 1950s using a decisional method, Edward Banfield concluded that the influence of the mayor was somewhat limited and that he or she typically became involved in decisions after they were made. Most important, the mayor tended to avoid controversial (or fragile)

decisions and waited until the various interest groups had ac-
commodated one another before making his or her position
clear and felt.[1]

This study is consistent with Banfield's conclusions about
the role of mayors in controversial decisions. Even though three
of the programs discussed involve decision making at the city
level, the mayors are perceived either as in opposition to the
programs, as reported in Table 9–1 regarding the City Community Action Program, or as unimportant in decisions regarding
the Program. Mayors do not appear in the Model Cities and
General Revenue Sharing regressions.

One problem of social science research deals with multicol-
linearity, ". . . the situation in which some or all of the independent variables are highly intercorrelated."[2] Consequently,
correlation matrices are presented after each regression of the
independent variables. Only the statistically significant rs will
be discussed. The ideal, but rarely achieved, situation is to have
no significant rs among the independent variables. Table 9–2
presents the intercorrelations of the independent variables in
the regression for the city Community Action Program.

The only significant intercorrelation among the independent variables in the regression equation is between city population and percent nonwhite. There is no significant
intercorrelation between any of the other independent variables
explaining output for the city Community Action Program.

Table 9–2 Product-Moment Correlation Among
Independent Variables Explaining Output
for the Community Action Program

	2	3	4	5
1. Percent nonwhite	.279	.394*	.162	.252
2. Percent unemployed		−.119	.145	−.092
3. City population			.091	.108
4. Importance of neighborhood groups				−.213
5. Decisional influence of mayor				—

* = p .05

In summary, when selected community variables are regressed on output for the city Community Action Program, certain demographic variables, especially percent unemployed and percent nonwhite, are most important in explaining variance. There is a strong, significant and direct relationship between these independent variables and grants for the Community Action Program. Of the remaining variables in the study, only two variables, the decisional influence of the mayor and the importance of neighborhood groups, are important, and they are related inversely to output.

MODEL CITIES PROGRAM

Table 9–3 presents the regression of community variables on the amount of the Model Cities Planning Grant.

Table 9–3 is the final in a series of 5 regressions to determine community variables related to spending for Model Cities. It was more difficult to explain grants for Model Cities using community variables because Model Cities was very different from the Community Action Program. Model Cities gave the mayor and the mayor's associates overall control. The Community Action Program provided for the establishment of Community Action Agencies outside of city government.

The Community Action Program encouraged broad citizen participation. Model Cities stressed a more centralized ap-

Table 9–3   Multiple Regression of Community Variables
on Amount of First Year Model Cities Planning Grant,
May 1969 to June 1971[a]

	Beta	R Square	Adjusted R Square
Percent nonwhite in 1970	.427*	.224	.224
Businessmen and business organizations	−.385*	.370	.338
		Total equation significant at .05	

* = p .05
[a] Model Cities Planning Grant Variable transformed by Log 10

proach to problem solving. The establishment of goals, objectives, and programs to implement these objectives and the development of measures of program benefits were all a part of the Model Cities program. The Model Cities program was aimed at changing the city bureaucracy from within, and therefore stressed bureaucratic and organizational variables not used in this study. The Community Action Program, on the other hand, was developed, in part, to mobilize community residents through a self help and community action strategy.

Clearly, Model Cities was not a program where decisions were made on the basis of broad community participation. Compared with the Community Action Program, Model Cities did not encourage the development of neighborhood groups. As an experiment in the application of new planning technologies to social problems, Model Cities embodied an elitist approach to social change. It is not surprising that the final regression equation can explain only 34 percent of the total adjusted variance.

As with the City Community Action Program, demographic and leadership variables are related to grants for the City Model Cities Program. There is a direct and significant relationship between percentage nonwhite and grants for both the City Community Action Program and Model Cities Program. Also, in Model Cities, a program that was funded through City Hall, the importance of businessmen and business organizations was inversely related to the amount of the Model Cities grant.

Table 9–4 shows that the two variables that explain variance in the amount of the grant for Model Cities are not signifi-

Table 9–4   Product-Moment Correlations
Among Independent Variables Explaining
Amount of the Model Cities Planning Grant

	2
1. Percent nonwhite	−.121
2. Businessmen	−

cantly intercorrelated. In other words, they have separate effects in explaining the variance of the dependent variable.

In summary, the Model Cities Planning Grant, representative of Creative Federalism, has determinants similar to another program under Creative Federalism, the City Community Action Program. Both are affected by demographic variables and leadership variables. However, with the variables employed in this study, a greater amount of variance can be explained for the Community Action Program than for Model Cities.

SOCIAL SERVICES UNDER GENERAL REVENUE SHARING

Allocations for social services under General Revenue Sharing, representing the New Federalism, comprise the last program studied at the city level. Table 9–5 contains the last of five regressions of community variables on allocations under General Revenue Sharing. It should be remembered that studies discussed in Chapter 5 consistently reported that only a small percentage (2 percent) of General Revenue Sharing funds were allocated by cities for social services.

Table 9–5 Multiple Regression of Community Variables on Social Service Allocations Under General Revenue Sharing, January 1972 to June 1974

Community variable	Beta	R Square	Adjusted R Square
Importance of neighborhood organizations	.860***	.171	.171
Importance of the problem of social improvement and welfare	.754***	.342	.309
Importance of church organizations	.601***	.520	.470
Percent unemployed in 1970	−.442*	.622	.559
Percent nonwhite in 1970	−.379	.675	.598
Decentralization	.201	.698	.603
	Total equation significant at .01		

*** = p .001
 ** = p .01
  * = p .05

The independent variables explain 60 percent of the adjusted variation among cities in allocations for social services under General Revenue Sharing. When voluntary association type variables are considered, the importance of neighborhood organizations varies directly with allocations for social service made under General Revenue Sharing (Beta = .860***). Similarly, the importance of church organizations varies directly with the amount of money allocated to social services (Beta = .601**). Spending for social services also varies directly with leaders' concern with the problem of social improvement and welfare (Beta = .754***).

However, spending was inversely related to the two demographic measures, the percent unemployed in 1970 and the percent nonwhite in 1970. Cities with a smaller percentage of unemployed and nonwhite persons tended to spend *more* for social services under General Revenue Sharing, while cities with a higher percentage of unemployed and nonwhite persons tended to spend *less* for social services for the poor and aged. Allocations for social services are also directly related to decentralization, although the relationship is weak and not significant.

In general, spending for social services, when there are not federal controls, is confined to a relatively small number of communities. In communities where there are some allocations for social welfare services, there is a value base among the leadership that recognizes that social welfare is an important problem, and there are active neighborhood organizations and church groups. Allocations are inversely related to need, as measured by two demographic variables, percent unemployed in 1970 and percent nonwhite in 1970.

Table 9–6 shows the Product-Moment Correlations among the independent variables explaining expenditures for social services under General Revenue Sharing. Two significant intercorrelations, between decentralization and percent nonwhite and decentralization and percent unemployed, appear in this table. In other words, more decentralized cities, which are generally larger, have a higher percentage of unemployed and

Table 9–6   Product-Moment Correlations
Among Independent Variables Explaining Output
for Social Services Under General Revenue Sharing

	2	3	4	5	6
1. Importance of welfare	.156	−.057	.219	.465*	.151
2. Neighborhood organizations		.409*	.214	.092	.231
3. Church organizations			.046	−.030	−.169
4. Percent unemployed in 1970				.084	.364*
5. Percent nonwhite in 1970					.501**
6. Decentralization					—

** = p .01
 * = p .05

nonwhite residents. As could be expected, neighborhood and
church organizations are also intercorrelated. Finally, as could
be expected, the importance of welfare is significantly related to
the percent nonwhite.

When General Revenue Sharing and the City Community
Action Program are compared, there are important differences
in the type, strength, and direction of association of the independent variables. The difference is between programs where
allocations for social welfare are directly related to indexes of
need (Community Action Program), and those where allocations are directly related to community interest groups (Revenue Sharing). Under General Revenue Sharing, allocations for
social services are directly and significantly related to the importance of social welfare, the importance of neighborhood
groups, and the support of church organizations. The Revenue
Sharing Program, when allocations are studied, is fulfilling its
purpose of being responsive to local community groups and
values.

This specific instance illustrates a more general policy
problem facing those concerned with the organized, rational,
and integrated delivery of social welfare services responsive to
social problems. The policy problem involves the conflict between the planned and usually centralized development of a
rational social service system based on need, on the one hand,
and the provision of services based on community values and

interest group pressures, on the other. This dilemma has been identified by many scholars, including Theodore Lowi in his book, *The End of Liberalism.* [3]

In his book, Lowi describes the development of the market system. Lowi feels that the market did not work in the economic sphere, but it was applied to the political sphere. The result was what he calls interest group liberalism, the guiding philosophy in America since the Great Depression. Decisions under interest group liberalism are based solely on the power, skill, and motivation of the interest groups that are drawn to issues. For Lowi, public policy, the court system, and much of the economy is controlled by interest groups. Since there are no universally accepted prescriptions, there is a crisis of authority in our society. Lowi feels that public policy cannot be based solely on interest groups and local community values.

These concerns are at the heart of the issue surrounding the most appropriate relationship between the federal government and the states and localities. Is it appropriate for the federal government to provide conditional grant-in-aid programs, based on national goals and some identifiable need, and operated under continuing federal supervision? This approach has been generally favored by humanitarians. However the humanitarian approach can be associated with centralization of power and authority and with decisions based on rational technologies. This approach is a potential threat to community participation and ultimately, to individual freedom.

The individualist approach to federalism was historically exemplified by Early Federalism and, at present, by the New Federalism. Under General Revenue Sharing, local communities, based on their values and the actors that become important around specific issues, determine public policy. The free market, as applied to decisions in governmental policy, or pluralism, prevails. Interest groups are important instead of expert and rational analyses of needs and alternative solutions. The risk of this approach is that community decision making can be controlled by powerful interest groups and result in policies which do not meet human needs. However, individualists feel that pluralism preserves freedom and democracy.

In summary, when factors influencing community decision making for programs under Creative Federalism are compared to the factors operating under New Federalism, important distinctions can be discovered. Even though all programs are responsive to measures chosen from leadership factors and the political and voluntary association factors, programs under Creative Federalism are more responsive to need, as measured by percent nonwhite and percent unemployed. Allocations for social services, under General Revenue Sharing, a program under the New Federalism, are related inversely to need, as measured by the percent nonwhite and the percent unemployed. To a greater extent, allocations under General Revenue Sharing is directly related to voluntary association activity and to leadership groups.

THE COUNTY COMMUNITY ACTION PROGRAM, THE COUNTY POVERTY PROGRAM, AND THE TOTAL POVERTY PROGRAM

These three measures are different from the measures of the spending for the City Community Action Program, the Model Cities Program, and Social Services under General Revenue Sharing. The County Community Action Program measures only nonmunicipal spending. It is on a different level of government and is responsive to a larger and perhaps substantively different consumer group. As will be shown, the regression for the County Community Action Program includes a greater number of political and leadership groups than did previous regressions. It is clear that decision making on the county level is somewhat different from decision making on the city level.

The two other programs, the total County Poverty Program and the totals for the City Poverty Program and the county Poverty Program, also are different from the previous programs studied. These measures include grants for categorical grant-in-aid type of programs. Head Start, Neighborhood Youth Corps, Upward Bound, and so forth, were all very specific programs under the Poverty Program. They were available to communities that applied for them and agreed to operate them consistent with federal objectives and specific federal operating guidelines. In contrast to the early days of the Community Action Program, where communities had substantial decision making power in the selection of programs operating on the local level, the Poverty Program measures include programs dictated totally by the federal government.

In the regressions that follow for the County Poverty Totals and for all Poverty Totals, it becomes more difficult to explain spending patterns with community-type variables of the sort employed in this study. The regression for the City Community Action Program explained 60 percent of the adjusted variance. It was possible to explain 60 percent of the adjusted variance of allocations for social services under revenue sharing. Community variables explain 70 percent of the adjusted variance in the County Community Action Program. All of these regression equations are significant at the .01 level. However, when the total County Poverty Program is considered, only 26 percent of the adjusted variance is explained. Similarly, community type variables can only explain 26 percent of the adjusted variance of the total Poverty Program, at the .05 level of significance.

Table 9–7 shows the community variables that explain policy output for the county Community Action Program.

In Table 9–7, four independent variables explain 70 percent of the total adjusted variance in the amount spent for the County Community Action Program. The first two independent variables are political-type factors, and they explain over 75 percent of the total variance explained. Communities whose leaders were more concerned with the importance of parks, recreation, and sports spent more for their County Community Action Program grant. The importance of professional organizations (the bar association, the medical association, and so

Table 9–7   Multiple Regression of Community Variables
on Total Amount of County Community Action Grant,
November 1964 to December 1965[a]

	Beta	R Square	Adjusted R Square
Domination of Democratic party in one-party communities	.504**	.371	.371
Importance of Republicans	−.413**	.495	.469
Importance of parks, recreation, and sports	.474**	.575	.534
Importance of professional organizations	−.458**	.737	.693
		Total equation significant at .001	

** = p .01
[a]County Community Action Variable transformed by Log 10

forth) was inversely related to spending for the County Community Action Program.

Table 9–8 shows the intercorrelations for the independent variables explaining the size of the County Community Action grant. There is only one significant correlation: parks and recreation with professional organizations.

In general, the County Community Action Program regression indicates the importance of political factors. In this case, the domination of the Democratic party and the importance of Republicans explain over 75 percent of the total variance explained by the variables in the equation.

Table 9–8   Product-Moment Correlations of Independent
Variables Explaining County Community Action Grant

	2	3	4
1. Importance of parks, recreation	.420*	−.202	−.163
2. Importance of professional organizations		−.328	.004
3. Importance of Republicans			.063
4. Domination of Democrats			—

* = p .05

Table 9–9 is a multiple regression of community variables on the total grant on the county level for all Poverty Programs. This total includes spending for conditional grant-in-aid type of programs, such as Neighborhood Youth Corps, available to communities under the Economic Opportunities Act at the county level. The regression reported in Table 9–9 is last in a series of five regressions.

Only 26 percent of the total adjusted variance can be explained with community type variables to result in an equation that is significant at the .05 percent level. Of the three variables, two are political type variables. Both the percent vote for the Democratic party in the 1960 Presidential Election and a score based on factor analysis on the "political" factor are related directly to increased spending for the County Poverty Program. A demographic factor, the change in the population from 1960 to 1970, also was included in the equation.

Table 9–10 shows that there are no significant intercorrelations among the independent variables explaining output for the County Poverty Program.

When the City and County Poverty Programs are combined, it is difficult to use community type variables to explain a large amount of variance. Table 9–11 shows that only two variables could be identified that could explain some variance

Table 9–9   Multiple Regression of Community Variables
on Amount of Total County Poverty Program,
November 1964 to December 1965[a]

	Beta	R Square	Adjusted R Square
Change in population from 1960 to 1970	.477*	.209	.209
Percent vote for Democratic party in 1960 presidential election	.312	.271	.234
Factor score on "political" factor	.349	.333	.262
	Total equation significant at .05		

* = p .05
[a]Total County Poverty Program Variable transformed by Log 10

Table 9–10   Product-Moment Correlation
of Independent Variables Explaining Amount
of Total County Poverty Program

	2	3
1. Change in population from 1960 to 1970	.160	–.358
2. Percent Democratic vote in 1960		–.098
3. Factor score on "political" factor		—

in all Poverty totals and yield an equation significant at the .05 level. One of these two, which explains over half of the variance explained, is the importance of the Democratic party.

Table 9–12 shows that there is no significant correlation between the two independent variables used to explain spending for the total Poverty Program on the city and county levels.

Table 9–13 shows the amount of variance explained in selected regressions where each regression is significant at least

Table 9–11   Multiple Regression of Community Variables
on All Poverty Totals, November 1964 to December 1965[a]

	Beta	R Square	Adjusted R Square
Black organizations in the Poverty Program	.422*	.150	.150
Importance of Democratic party	.385	.297	.262
		Total equation significant at .05	

* = p .05
[a] All Poverty Totals variable transformal by Log 10

Table 9–12   Product-Moment Correlations
Among Independent Variables Explaining
All Poverty Levels

	2
1. Black organizations	.092
2. Democratic party	—

Table 9–13   Final R Square and Adjusted R Square
for Selected Programs

Program	R Square	Adjusted R Square
City Community Action Program	.678	.603
City Revenue Sharing Program	.698	.603
County Community Action Program	.737	.693
County Poverty Program	.333	.262
City and County Poverty Program	.297	.262

at the .05 level, employing community-type variables. The decreasing utility of these types of variables for programs that include categorical-type grants, such as the Poverty Program, is clearly evident.

LIMITATIONS OF THE STUDY

The guiding interest of the study has been to discover factors that have explanatory power in terms of social welfare grants in different community based programs. The emphasis here is on the initial decision to participate and early experience with the programs. The concern lies with public policy decisions and the factors that determine the making of these decisions, not with their implementation.

In other words, knowing that a city participates in the Community Action Program, in Model Cities, or in social services under Revenue Sharing provides us with some information. In a general sense, it is assumed that a city carries out the broad intent of the legislation. However, in block grant type programs, especially in the early years, there was little federal control. The specific way money actually was spent under the broad heading of Community Action Program or Model Cities or Revenue Sharing is not measured in this research. It is of concern that a community decided to participate in programs that had the reduction of poverty as their major purpose. However, this research does not deal with policy impacts or with the effects of these programs. What they accomplished has been the subject of other works.

Past studies that attempted to explain why some cities spent more than others in various programs have measured policy output over *a long period of time.* Thus, the studies by Aiken and Alford,[4] for example, looked at the total experience that a city had with public housing and urban renewal. In some programs, this experience might have involved policy output for a program totaled over 25 years.[5] Similarly, other studies that attempted to explain why some cities spend more per capita than others compare cities' budgets, which are the result of a series of decisions taken over a long period of time. These decisions are certainly the result, to some extent, of community factors of the type used in the present study. However, they also might be the result of bureaucratic factors that, within certain parameters, vary independently from community input. Once a program becomes established, it has a life of its own. The means become the ends. The emphasis is on expanding the program and protecting it within the public bureaucracy. Inter-organizational considerations become primary, and the factors that were originally significant in helping a community to get into a program are replaced by a total different set of factors.[6]

The results of research using the method of looking at policy outputs over a long period of time tend to confirm the importance of bureaucratic factors. In a recent article, Aiken and Alford suggest that the size and sophistication of a city's bureaucracy and grantsmanship ability are the major factors that affect policy output for federal-local programs.[7] In order to minimize the effect of these factors, the present study limits itself to the first two years each program was available from the federal government.

In other words, the development and early experience with social policy involves different processes from its administration. It is probable that as new programs become available and are given national publicity, a range of community forces and interests will attempt to influence decision centers. The present study is designed to isolate the effect of community factors in public decision making. However, after a certain period of time, a totally new set of factors relating to program growth might take precedence. Public and community interest die down. The bureaucracy, national, state, and local becomes more significant. Community variables are replaced with bureaucratic variables to explain program growth. Past studies have failed to separate the stages of policy development and policy administration and implementation.

Both approaches—studying determinants of policy development and studying determinants of policy implementation—are valid. However, they should be distinguished. This distinction in the stages of policy development and implementation suggest that those concerned with the history of public policy once a community has decided to implement a program should pay less attention to community type variables of the sort used in this study and more attention to organizational analysis.

The present study deals with policy outputs of a very specific kind. Generally, they are separable goods and involve fragile decisions. It is presumed, although not proven (and beyond the scope of this study), that there is some element of redistribution of public money, time, and energy from middle- and upper-class concerns to lower-class interests.

Past studies of policy output have concentrated on more general questions. A typical question might be, "Why does city A have a higher city budget than city B?" The focus was on isolating community type factors that varied with differences in per capita city spending. However, different types of policy outputs may have different determinants *within the same city.* For example, although a city might be highly decentralized in general, there might be a high degree of centralization around a specific issue, such as programs to benefit the poor. The conclusions of this study relate to social welfare services for the poor and might not be transferable to other policy areas. More public goods, such as reduction of air pollution or fluoridation of the water, and less fragile decisions might have different determinants.

Also, the historical section of this book has described the

national mood during the 1960s. There was a massive resurgence of interest in social problems. For example, in October 1965, 60 percent of the respondents in a Harris Poll approved of the President's handling of the War on Poverty. In less than one year, the mood of the country had shifted. In September 1966, only 41 percent approved of the President's handling of the War on Poverty.[8] The spirit of the early 1960s was one of optimism. Social engineering, funded by the federal government and operated by communities, could be successful.[9] It was felt that poverty would be eliminated in America. Budget deficits, the need to set priorities between competing national programs, the politics of scarcity, inflation and unemployment, the dwindling supply of natural resources, and other concerns of the 1970s were not high in the collective consciousness during the 1960s. The factors that were related to program development during the 1960s might not be as important in other periods.

Finally, the study was made of middle-sized communities. It was felt that community variables would be most evident in middle-sized communities. The generality of the results of the empirical study, although consistent with the philosophical and historical analysis, may be limited to comparable sized communities.

CONCLUSION

The programs used in this study represent three different types of federalism. The Poverty Program measures include programs characteristic of the conditional grant-in-aid program, which expanded under Cooperative Federalism. In a grant-in-aid program the federal government makes specific grants for specific purposes and dictates the implementation of these programs on the local level.

The Community Action Program is most representative of Creative Federalism. In programs characteristic of Creative Federalism, the federal government develops broad goals and objectives and provides local communities with decision making power over the type of program to be created. General Revenue Sharing, a program under the New Federalism, gives localities total decision making authority over the type and content of all programs with almost no federal involvement.

Of these programs, it is least possible to explain expenditures under the Poverty Program with community type variables. This is because there is very little community input. The variables that are most significant in these programs are political type variables, especially the importance of the Democratic party. When conditional grant-in-aid type of programs are considered, communities with a strong Democratic party orientation (when there was a national Democratic administration) received larger grants than communities without Democrats important in community decision making.

When programs under Creative Federalism are considered, a combination of need and community influence factors explain the amount of local expenditures. By setting national goals, the federal government insured that expenditures were responsive to need, but allowed for local input in decisions about how monies were to be spent.

Finally, when there are no federal controls, as under General Revenue Sharing, allocation decisions are made primarily on the constellation of values and interest groups on the local level. Allocations are made regardless of any objective criteria of need, and under Social Services for General Revenue Sharing, allocations were inversely related to the percent nonwhite and the percent employed.

Table 9–14 presents the final regressions for three programs. The Beta scores are listed in terms of specific community variables, not in the order they appeared in the final regression.

Table 9–14 confirms the major assumption of this study, that community variables differ in the way they explain spending for social welfare services under different conceptions of federalism. Thus, two demographic measures that can be seen as indexes of need vary directly with grants for the City Community Action Program and inversely with allocations for so-

Table 9–14 Multiple Regressions of Community Variables for Three Programs

Community type variables	Block grants Creative federalism City Community Action 60 percent Betas	General revenue sharing New federalism Social Services 60 percent Betas	Grant-in-aid Cooperative federalsim Poverty Program 26 percent Betas
Final Adjusted R Square			
Demographic			
Percent unemployed	.69***	−.44*	
Percent nonwhite	.47*	−.38	
City population	.29		
Political and voluntary organizations			
Neighborhood organization	−.51***	.86***	
Church organization		.60**	
Democratic party			.39
Black organizations			.42*
Leadership			
Mayor	−.30		
Values			
Social welfare		.75**	
Centralization			
Decentralization		.20	
Structure of government			
Total equation significant at	.01	.01	.05

*** = p .001
** = p .01
* = p .05

cial services under Revenue Sharing. The importance of neighborhood organizations varies inversely with grants under the City Community Action Program and directly with allocations for social services under General Revenue Sharing. When an effort is made to employ community variables to explain grants for the Poverty Program, a grant-in-aid type program on the city and county level, only 26 percent of the adjusted variance is explained.

Finally, one purpose of this study was to identify the community factors, from the model of community factors presented in Chapter 6, that were most important in explaining grants for social welfare at the local level. Table 9–15 presents the Betas of all the previous regressions by community factors. As in Table 9–14 the Beta scores are listed in terms of specific community variables, not in the order in which they appeared in the final regression.

When the type of community variables important in explaining output for all programs is considered, political and voluntary organization type variables occur most frequently. Demographic variables appeared less frequently. Only two leadership variables are important, and both of them are inversely related to allocations for social services for the poor on the community level. The importance that leaders attach to various social problems was also important and significant. Decentralization was not as important as originally expected in explaining allocations for social welfare. Finally, the structure of urban government does not appear to affect allocations in the area of social welfare.

Of all the measures, the leadership variables produced the most unexpected results. The mayor, often seen as a key to the urban policy process, was little in evidence. Also unimportant were newspapers and unions (which were entered into several regressions), often identified with humanitarian concerns. In general, the leadership variables, in the area of social welfare programs for the poor, are not as important or as positive as originally expected.

Table 9–15 Multiple Regressions of Community Variables for All Programs

Community variables	City Community Action Program	Model Cities	Revenue Sharing	County Community Action Program	County Poverty Program	All Poverty Program
Demographic						
Percent nonwhite	.47*	.43*	-.38			
Percent unemployed	.69***		-.44*			
City population	.29					
Population change					.48*	
Political and voluntary organizations						
Neighborhood groups	-.51***		.86***			
Republican party				-.41**		
Domination of Democratic party				.50**		
Percent vote democratic					.31	
Democratic party						.39
Political factor					.35	
Church organizations			.60**			

	.01	.05	.01	.001	.05	.05
Professional organizations						
Black organizations				-.46**		.42
Leadership						
Mayor	-.30					
Businessmen		-.39*				
Values						
Social welfare			.75***			
Parks and recreation				.47**		
Centralization						
Decentralization			.20			
Structure of government						
Reform government						
Total equation significant at	.01	.05	.01	.001	.05	.05

*** = p .001
** = p .01
* = p .05

189

NOTES

1. Edward C. Banfield. *Political Influence.* New York: Free Press, 1961.

2. Norman H. Nie, C. Hadlai Hull, Jean G. Jenkins, Karin Steinbrenner, and Dale H. Bent, *Statistical Package for the Social Sciences.* second ed. New York: McGraw-Hill, 1975, p. 38.

3. Theodore Lowi. *The End of Liberalism.* New York: W. W. Norton, 1969.

4. Michael Aiken and Robert R. Alford. "Community Structure and Innovation: Public Housing, Urban Renewal and the War on Poverty." In *Comparative Community Politics.* Terry N. Clark, ed., New York: Halsted Press, 1977.

5. Ibid.

6. See, for example, Anthony Downs. *Inside Bureaucracy.* Boston: Little, Brown, 1967.

7. Aiken and Alford.

8. James L. Sundquist, *Politics and Policy: The Eisenhower, Kennedy, and Johnson Years.* Washington, D.C.: The Brookings Institution, 1968, p. 497.

9. Peter Marris, and Martin Rein. *Dilemmas of Social Reform: Poverty and Community Action in the United States.* New York: Atherton Press, 1969.

Chapter 10

SUMMARY AND CONCLUSIONS

INTRODUCTION

To give to the local communities total control of decision making for social welfare is against the best interests of the poor and others with special needs. It has been true historically. It remains true today for programs in which municipalities have the freedom to establish goals, means, and priorities. The reason is in part that those served by social welfare programs generally are not powerful enough on the community level to prevail in the competition among strong and skillful interest groups. Policy in the area of social welfare, if it is to be responsive to the poor and to others needing social service, must involve extra-local controls on the delivery of services at the community level.

This study has looked at community decision making for social welfare from a philosophical, historical, and empirical perspective. Philosophically, a distinction was made between those with an individualistic orientation and those with a humanitarian orientation. Individualists blame social problems on the client. They feel that those suffering from problems, and not government, should be responsible for the solution of these problems. Individualists have favored a pluralistic model for public decision making.

Humanitarians have tended to attribute the cause of social problems more to the structure of society than have individualists. Therefore, humanitarians are more likely to look to society and to government for the solution of social problems. Humanitarians generally support federal intervention and control in social policy. They feel that when policy is made solely on the basis of the interaction of interest groups, those with relatively little power at the community level do not benefit.

DIFFERENT APPROACHES TO FEDERALISM

Especially since the Great Depression, there has been a growing federal presence in all areas of public policy. In contrast, during the early years of our country's development, the states had powers not specifically reserved for the federal government. Under Early Federalism, the role of the federal government was more limited. Social welfare provisions were furnished by the private sector, the localities, and the states.

As the nation grew in size and complexity and its communities became more interdependent, a larger federal role was needed. Cooperative Federalism, which started during the Great Depression, involved the intermingling of federal and state functions. The grant-in-aid system expanded during Cooperative Federalism. Under grants-in-aid, the federal government established goals and programs to implement them. States had the option of participating in programs. A consequence of this type of approach and of other policies characteristic of Cooperative Federalism was a dramatic increase in federal power and control.

The Creative Federalism of Lyndon Johnson can be seen as a reaction to the centralization of earlier periods. Although federal monies were still used, the states and localities gained more decision making powers. With Creative Federalism, the block grant was extensively used. Under this approach the federal government establishes the broad goals of a policy, and states and localities have some freedom in selecting programmatic means to implement these goals. Decision making is decentralized to the states and municipalities. The early years of the Community Action Program of the War on Poverty and of the Model Cities Program are often cited as examples of programs typical of Creative Federalism. The early years of these programs provide an example of community decision making within the boundaries of federal goals. However, despite the appearance of local control, federal power gradually reasserted itself. In the later years of the Community Action Program, for example, $6 out of every $10 were spent for national priority programs encouraged by the Federal Office of Economic Opportunity.

With the Nixon Administration came the New Federalism. The purest expression of the New Federalism is General Revenue Sharing. In contrast to programs under Creative Federalism, monies regularly are returned to states and localities. No grant applications are required from localities. No federal goals are established relating to the programmatic purposes of the grant. There is minimal federal direction of how the money can be spent. In contrast to programs under Creative Federalism, localities do not have to establish new departments or organizations to administer funds under General Revenue Sharing. The major requirement is that states and municipalities report regularly and publicly how they allocated their General Revenue Sharing funds. Community decision making seems most possible under this type of program.

Although the problems associated with big government are generally recognized, there has been a growing fear among social workers and others about the fate of clients when the federal government is removed from all control of social policy. Many social welfare professionals are opposed to this trend toward local control and fear its consequences for social welfare.

The empirical study is an effort to identify community factors that are related to spending under differing conceptions of federalism for social welfare programs. The Poverty Program, representative of Cooperative Federalism, the Community Action Program and Model Cities, characteristic of Creative Federalism, and General Revenue Sharing, typical of the New Federalism, were selected for further analysis.

COMMUNITY ACTION PROGRAM AND MODEL CITIES

The Community Action Program was an early example of a federal grant to a community. In the past, grants normally went to the states. The Community Action Program was a block-type grant. The federal government established the broad goals. The Community Action Program was implemented on the local level through a newly established organization created outside of City Hall. This new agency included representatives of major institutions, such as the local government, the schools, community leaders, and the poor. Its purpose was to develop and administer programs to implement the national goals. During their early years, many Community Action Programs encouraged community involvement.

Model Cities's differed from the Community Action Program in several important respects. There were still federal goals, but planning instead of community action was the major method employed to create a "model city." In contrast to the Community Action Program, Model Cities was funded through city government. Model Cities' approach was to attempt to promote change from within City Hall; the Community Action Program tried to achieve change from without. If municipalities wanted to participate in Model Cities, they had to prepare an elaborate proposal. If this proposal was funded, cities received a one year planning grant and then yearly implementation grants.

GENERAL REVENUE SHARING

General Revenue Sharing returns federal monies to states and municipalities. Municipalities can use this money to reduce their property tax; they can deposit it in the bank to earn interest; they can use it to reduce their debt; or they can spend it for local services, including social services for the poor and aged. Monies are distributed regularly from the federal government, and one of the few requirements is that localities report how they allocated their funds.

Early experience with the program indicates that municipalities allocate the majority of their funds for police protection. However, there is some indication that their reporting is misleading, and that the money tends to be spent more for general government than for other purposes. When allocations for social services for the poor and aged are considered, only about 2 percent of the total amount of money provided under General Revenue Sharing is allocated and spent for this purpose on the municipal level.

FACTORS RELATED TO COMMUNITY DECISION MAKING

In order to study the factors related to community decision making under different kinds of federalism, six community factors were selected from an input-output model of community decision making. These factors included demographic and economic variables, political parties and voluntary associational activity, leadership, values and cultural characteristics, centralization, and the structure of local government. Certain measures of these variables were then selected in order to determine which were most significant in explaining variation in the amount of the grants for social welfare on the local level under the programs considered.

An *ex post facto* research design was used. Measures of the six community factors were the independent variables, while the amount of grants for the programs were the dependent variables. Since interval data were used, the major statistical technique was multiple regression analysis. R-Square and adjusted R-Square statistics are reported for each regression, along with correlation matrices of the independent variables.

The sample was drawn from the Permanent Community Study of the National Opinion Research Corporation. The sample used in the present study included 22 municipalities. In 1960, the municipalities had populations ranging between 85,000 and 310,000 persons. Four of the municipalities were suburbs; the remainder were central cities. Five were from the Northeast, six from the Midwest, four from the South, and seven from the West.

In each city, a questionnaire was administered to top leaders, such as the mayor, the president of the largest bank, the chairman of the Democratic party, and the head of the largest hospital drive. The interviews were conducted by the professional staff of the National Opinion Research Corporation. The questions dealt with each leader's opinions about the most important problems in the municipality and the actors who were important in these problems. In addition to the interviews, data from the *U.S. Census,* the *Municipal Yearbook,* and the *City and County Data Book* were used.

Data for the dependent variables were collected from publications of the Office of Economic Opportunity, the U.S. Department of Housing and Urban Renewal, and the Office of Revenue Sharing, U.S. Department of the Treasury.

Major Conclusions

The major conclusion of the study is that when social welfare programs for the poor on the local level are considered, there must be some nonlocal involvement directing municipalities to spend money in low income areas. In the absence of federal controls, allocations were made on the basis of interest group activity. Table 10–1 shows this general conclusion.

Table 10–1   The Basis of Allocations for Social Services
for the Poor Under Partial and Total Community Control

	Community Action Program Federal goals Local means (Betas)	General Revenue Sharing Local goals Local means (Betas)
Indices of need		
percentage nonwhite	+.47*	−.38
percentage unemployed	+.69***	−.44*
Interest groups		
Importance of neighborhood		
groups	−.51***	+.86***

*** = p .001
** = p .01
* = p .05

When the federal government establishes the goals and the means, community variables are not as successful in explaining variation in the size of the grant at the community level. The regression for the total Poverty Program, a conditional grant-in-aid program, on the city and county level, could explain only 26 percent of the adjusted variance significant at the .05 level. In contrast, the final regression for the City Community Action Program, a block grant program, explained 60 percent of the adjusted variance and the final regression for the city allocation for social services under Revenue Sharing explained 60 percent of the adjusted variance as well. Both regressions were significant at .01.

When the types of variables important in explaining grants for social welfare at the local level are considered, political and voluntary associational activity measures occurred most often. Demographic and leadership variables occurred somewhat less often. The leadership measures were inversely related to grants for social services. The importance that leaders attached to various problems also were important in explaining output for social welfare. Decentralization appeared least frequently and the measure of the structure of urban government did not appear in any of the reported regressions.

The study focuses on identifying community factors that were related to grants and allocations for social services for the poor under different types of federal funding mechanisms. It does not deal with the effectiveness of these programs or the impacts they have on the client groups. It is somewhat different from previous studies in the community decision making literature because it deals with only the first two years of each program. It is felt that the first two years are the time period of maximum community decision making. As a program becomes older and more established, more bureaucratic factors probably determine the amount of spending.

The stated goal of the New Federalism was to return power and decision making ability to the local communities. There is some indication that when the total General Revenue Sharing Program is considered, power and decision making ability were returned to the local politicians and city civil servants. When social services for the poor and aged are considered, allocations are responsive to community group and interest group pressures. However, these allocations occur in only a small percentage of the cities and are inversely related to indices of need.

Total local control might be needed and valuable for some purposes. But in an area such as social services for the poor, where there is neither widespread public understanding nor support, the total reliance on local decision making results in a substantial reduction of the level of services and allocations inversely related to need. This study supports the contention that for social services to be delivered on the local level, there must be some outside direction and control. The way in which this direction and control can be secured, while at the same time protecting community participation and individual freedom, appears to be one of the more critical problems facing social welfare professionals and the country.

INDEPENDENT VARIABLES— FUNDAMENTAL FACTORS IN COMMUNITY DECISION MAKING[1]

1. DEMOGRAPHIC AND ECONOMIC VARIABLES

CITYPOP
   City population, 1960, in thousands (i.e., 210.00 = 210,000)
   Source: CCDB '62, Table 6.
POP70T
   City Population in 1970
   Source: CCDB '73
POP6070T
   Change in population from 1960 to 1970
   (POP6070T = POP70T - CITYPOP)
PC60UNEM
   Percent Unemployed in 1959
   CCDB '62

[1]FAST DECK CODEBOOK, Revised January 26, 1973.

PC70UNEM
  Percent Unemployed in 1970
  CCDB '72
PC60NONW
  Percent Nonwhite in 1960
  CCDB '62
PC70NONW
  Percent Nonwhite in 1970
  CCDB '72

2. POLITICAL PARTIES AND VOLUNTARY ORGANIZATIONS

PCEDEMVOT
  Percent vote for Democratic party in 1960 presidential
  election for SMSA
  Source: CCDB '62, Table 3
PARTYDOM
  Identification of dominant party in one-party cities
        Dem = 1
        Rep = 3
        Neither = 2
IMDEM
  Closed-end reputational index for Democratic party
  across five issue areas. Constructed by summing an ac-
  tor's scores and dividing by the number of issue areas
IMREP
  Combined index for Republicans. Constructed the same
  as IMDEM
IMNBR
  Combined index for neighborhood groups. Constructed
  the same as IMDEM
FPOLITL
  Factor score on "political" factor based on factor analy-
  sis of closed-ended reputational questions

CHURCHPV

Decisional influence of churches, church groups, and religious leaders in the poverty program, based on ersatz decisional questions constructed by dividing the number of mentions for the actor in the issue area by the total number of mentions in the issue area

PROFESPV

Decisional measure of professional organization in the poverty program. Constructed the same as CHURCHPV

BLACKSPV

Decisional influence of Black organizations. Constructed the same as CHURCHPV

3. LEADERSHIP

BUSNESPV

Businessmen and business organizations, including U.S. Chamber of Commerce. Constructed the same as CHURCHPV

DCINMAYR

Decisional influence of the mayor across four issue areas, transformed by log (VAR + .01). Constructed by dividing number of mentions for the mayor by number of total mentions

4. VALUES

WELFARE

Importance of the problem of social improvement and welfare. Based on open-ended responses and constructed by adding together the total number of responses "very important" and "most important"

PRKSPORT

Importance of recreation, parks, culture, sports (includes construction of civic centers, auditoriums, and libraries) constructed the same as WELFARE

5. CENTRALIZATION

NEWDECEN

New index of decentralization. Based on ersatz decisional questions. Constructed by dividing the sum of actors mentioned in two or more issue areas by the sum of all distinct actors mentioned for the city

6. STRUCTURE OF MUNICIPAL GOVERNMENT

REFORMGV (this variable was not significant or powerful enough to be included in the final regressions)
Index of reform government, constructed by combining the following variables:

    a. Form of city government (council-manager = 1, all others = 0)
    b. Number of at-large council constituencies (over half = 1, less than half = 0)
    c. Type of election of councilmen (nonpartisan = 1, all others = 0)

Source: *Municipal Yearbook 1966*, Table 5

DEPENDENT VARIABLES[1]

LCTCADT

Recoded version of date city first received community action grant where $11/64 = 560$, $12/65 = 40$; monthly increments of 40; transformed by log 10

*LCTCAP

Amount of total city community action money, in thousands of dollars, November 1964 to December 1965; transformed by log 10.

*LCOCAP

Amount of total county community action grant, in thousands of dollars, November 1964 to December 1965; transformed by log 10.

*LCOPOVTO

Amount of total county poverty programs, in thousands of dollars. Not computed for cities 22, 30, and 40 all in Los Angeles County, November 1964 to December 1965; transformed by log 10.

---

[1]The asterisks indicate the variables used in the final study.

*LALCTCOT

All poverty totals, in thousands of dollars, November 1964 to December 1965; transformed by log 10.

LMODATE

Weighted date city received first year operating grant where 5/69 = 520 and 6/71 = 20 and +20 for each month; transformed by log 10.

*LMODPLAN

Amount of Model Cities planning grant, in thousands of dollars, May 1969 to June 1971 (amounts for first year only); transformed by log 10.

*LMODTOT

Total amount of Model Cities money, in thousands of dollars, May 1969 to December 1972; transformed by log 10.

*RSSOSPT

Expenditures for social services divided by total city expenditures under revenue sharing, January 1, 1972 to June 30, 1974. Includes expenditures reported for operating, maintenance, and capital expenses.

BIBLIOGRAPHY

Ableman vs. Booth, 62 U.S. (21 How.) 506 (1859).

Advisory Commission on Intergovernmental Relations. "Final Report of the Advisory Commission on Intergovernmental Relations." Washington, D.C.: U.S. Government Printing Office, 1955.

Advisory Commission on Intergovernmental Relations. "Periodic Congressional Reassessment of Federal Grants in Aid to State and Local Governments." Washington, D.C.: U.S. Government Printing Office, 1961.

Agger, Robert, Goldrich, Daniel, & Swanson, Bert. *The rulers and the ruled: Political power and impotence in American communities.* New York: John Wiley, 1964.

Aiken, Michael, & Alford, Robert R. Community structure and innovation: Public housing, urban renewal and the war on poverty. In Terry N. Clark (Ed.), *Comparative community politics.* Chicago, 1975 (mimeographed).

Aiken, Michael, & Mott, Paul (Eds.) *The structure of community power.* New York: Random House, 1970.

Anton, Thomas, J., Larkey, Patrick, Linton, Toni, Epstein, Joel, Fox, John, Townsend, Nancy, & Zawacki, Claudia. *Understanding the fiscal impact of general revenue sharing.* Ann Arbor, Mich.: Institute of Public Policy Studies, June 30, 1975.

Baker, Earl M., Stevens, Bernadette A., Schechter, Stephen L., Wright, Harlan A. *Federal grants, The national interest and state response: A review of theory and research.* Philadelphia: Temple University, Center for the Study of Federalism, p. 20.

Banfield, Edward C. *Political influence.* New York: Free Press, 1960.

Banfield, Edward C. *The unheavenly city.* New York: Little, Brown, 1970.

Blalock, Hubert M. *Social statistics.* New York: McGraw-Hill, 1972.

Bremner, Robert. *From the depths: The discovery of poverty in the United States.* New York: New York University Press, 1960.

Breul, Frank R., & Wade, Alan D. (Eds.) *Readings in social welfare policy and services.* Chicago: University of Chicago, School of Social Service Administration (mimeographed).

Brick, Yitzchak. The relation of vertical ties to community competence. Ph.D. dissertation, Brandeis University, February 1975.

Bureau of Labor Statistics. *Handbook of Labor Statistics 1931.* Published as Bulletin No. 541. Washington, D.C.: U.S. Government Printing Office, 1931.

Caputo, David A., & Cole, Richard L. *Urban politics and decentralization: The case of general revenue sharing.* New York: D. C. Heath and Co., 1974.

Caputo, David A., & Cole, Richard L. Initial decisions in general revenue sharing. *Municipal Yearbook 1974.* Washington, D.C.: International City Management Association, 1974.

City of Clinton versus Cedar Rapids and Missouri River Railroad Company, 24, Iowa: 455 (1868).

Clark, Jane. *The rise of a new federalism: Federal-state cooperation in the United States.* New York: Columbia University Press, 1938.

Clark, Terry N. "Can you cut a budget pie?" *Policy and Politics,* December 1974, **3**, 3–32.

Clark, Terry N. *Cities differ—but how and why?: Inputs to national urban policy from research on decision-making in 51 American municipalities.* Report to Office of Policy Development and Research, U.S. Department of Housing and Urban Development, September, 1975, pp. 7–9.

Clark, Terry N. *Community power and policy outputs: A review of urban research.* Beverly Hills, Calif.: Sage Publications, 1973.

Clark, Terry N. Community structure, decision-making, budget expenditures, and urban renewal in 51 American communities. *American Sociological Review,* August 1968, **33**, 576–93.

Clark, Terry N. *Community structure and decision-making: Comparative analyses.* Scranton, Pa.: Chandler Publishing, 1968.

Clark, Terry N. Leadership in American cities: Resources, interchanges, and the press. Unpublished manuscript, Chicago, June 1973.

Clark, Terry N. "Money and the cities." Draft paper, Chicago, 1975.

Cohen, Wilbur. "The new federalism: Theory, practice, problems." *National Journal,* special report, March 1973, p. 14.

Coll, Blanche D. *Perspectives in public welfare: A history.* Washington, D.C. U.S. Government Printing Office, 1969.

Comptroller General of the United States, Report to the Congress. Revenue sharing: Its use by and impact on local governments. Washington, D.C.: U.S. Government Printing Office, April 25, 1974.

Comptroller General of the United States, Report to the Subcommittee on Intergovernmental Relations Committee on Government Operations, U.S. Senate. Case studies of revenue sharing in 26 local governments. Washington, D.C.: U.S. Government Printing Office, July 21, 1975.

Corwin, Edward S. *The twilight of the supreme court.* New Haven: Yale University Press, 1934.

Crain, Robert L., Katz, Elihu, & Rosenthal, Donald B. *The politics of community conflict: The fluoridation decision.* Indianapolis: Bobbs-Merrill, 1967.

Dahl, Robert A. *Who governs? Democracy and power in an American city.* New Haven, Conn.: Yale University Press, 1961.

Davidson, Roger. Creative federalism and the war on poverty. *Poverty and Human Resource Abstracts,* November-December 1966, **1,** 5-14.

Derthick, Martha. *The influence of federal grants: Public assistance in Massachusetts.* Cambridge, Mass.: Harvard University Press, 1970.

Donovan, John C. *The politics of poverty.* New York: Pegasus, 1967.

Downes, Brian T. (Ed.) *Cities and suburbs: Selected readings in local politics and public policy.* Belmont, Calif.: Wadsworth Publishing, 1971.

Downs, Anthony. *Inside bureaucracy.* Boston: Little, Brown, 1967.

Drucker, Peter F. *Age of discontinuity.* New York: Harper and Row, 1968.

Dry-Lands Research Institute. *The effects of general revenue sharing on ninety-seven cities in southern California.* University of California, Riverside, 1975.

Elazar, Daniel J. *American federalism: A view from the states.* New York: Thomas Y. Crowell Co., 1966.

Elazar, Daniel. *The American partnership.* Chicago: University of Chicago Press, 1962.

Gil, David. *Unravelling social policy: Theory, analysis, and political action towards social equality.* Cambridge, Mass.: Schenkman Publishing Company, 1973.

Goodwin, Richard. The shape of American politics. *Commentary,* June 1967, **43,** 25-40.

Greenstone, J. David, & Peterson, Paul E. *Race and authority in urban politics: Community participation and the war on poverty.* New York: Russell Sage, 1973.

Grodzins, Morton, Daniel J. Elazar (Ed.) *The American system: A new view of government in the United States.* Chicago: Rand McNally & Co., 1966.

Grønbjerg, Kirsten A. Mass society and the extension of welfare, 1960–1970. Ph.D. Thesis, Department of Sociology, University of Chicago, June 1974.

Hammer vs. **Dagenhart,** 247 U.S. 251 (1918).

Harbert, Anita S. Federal grants-in-aid: A study of demographic economic, and political factors and the capacity of states to benefit from grants. Ph.D. dissertation, Brandeis University, October 1974.

Hardcastle, David A. General revenue sharing and social work. *Social Work,* September 1973, **18,** 3–8.

Harrington, Michael. *The other America: Poverty in the United States.* Baltimore: Penguin Books, 1962.

Heller, Walter. *New dimensions of political economy.* Baltimore: Johns Hopkins Press, 1968.

Hofferbert, Richard I. Ecological development and policy change. *Midwest Journal of Political Science,* November 1966, **10,** 464–83.

Hofstadter, Richard. *Social Darwinism in American thought.* Boston: The Beacon Press, 1955.

Hunter, Floyd. *Community power structure: A study of decision makers.* Chapel Hill, N.C.: University of North Carolina Press, 1953.

Johnson, Claudius O., Castleberry, H. Paul, Ogden, Daniel M., Jr., Swanson, Thor. *American national government.* Fifth edition. New York: Thomas Y. Crowell Co., 1960, p. 124.

Kerlinger, Fred N., & Pedhazur, Elazar J. *Multiple regression in behavioral research.* New York: Holt, Rinehart and Winston, 1973.

Key, V. O. *The administration of federal grants to the states.* Chicago: Public Administration Service, 1937.

Lampman, Robert. *Ends and means of reducing income poverty.* Chicago: Markham Publishing, 1971.

Lampman, Robert J. "The low income population and economic growth," Joint Economic Committee, Congress of the United States, 86th Congress, 1st Session, Washington, D.C.: U.S. Government Printing Office, December 16, 1959.

Landrieu, Mayor Moon. Statement at the revenue sharing oversight hearings before the senate government operations subcommittee on intergovernmental relations. Washington, D.C., June 11, 1974.

Laumann, Edward O., Verbrugge, Lois M., & Pappi, Franz U. A causal modelling approach to the study of a community elite's influence structure. *American Sociological Review,* April 1974, **39,** 162–74.

Levitan, Sar A. *The great society's poor law: A new approach to poverty.* Baltimore: The Johns Hopkins Press, 1969.

Lowi, Theodore. *The end of liberalism.* New York: W. W. Norton, 1969.

Lyon, Larry. Community power and policy outputs: A question of relevance, in Roland Warren (ed.) *New Persepectives in the American Community: A Book of Readings.* Third Edition. Chicago: Rand McNally College Publishing Co., 1977, pp. 418–434.

Magill, Robert S., & Clark, Terry N. Community power and decision-making: Recent research and its policy implications. *Social Service Review,* March 1975, **49,** 33–45.

Magill, Robert S. Federalism, grants-in-aid, and social welfare policy, *Social Casework,* December, 1967, pp. 625–636.

Magill, Robert S. Joining formal voluntary associations and social action among the poor, *The Journal of Voluntary Action Research,* October, 1973, pp. 224–229.

Magill, Robert S. Who decides revenue sharing allocations? *Social Work,* July, 1977, pp. 297–300.

Marris, Peter, & Rein, Martin. *Dilemmas of social reform: Poverty and community action in the United States.* New York: Atherton Press, 1969.

Martin, Roscoe C. *The cities and the federal system.* New York: Atherton Press, 1965.

Massachusetts vs. **Mellon** 262 U.S. 447 (1923).

Miller, S. M., & Reissman, Frank. *Social class and social policy.* New York: Basic Books, 1968.

Miller, S. M., & Roby, Pamela. *The future of inequality.* New York: Basic Books, 1970.

Morlock, Laura A. Business interests, countervailing groups and the balance of influence in 91 cities. In Willis D. Hawley and Frederick M. Wirt (Eds.) *The Search for Community Power.* (2nd ed.) Englewood Cliffs, N.J.: Prentice-Hall, 1974.

Moynihan, Daniel. *Maximum feasible misunderstanding.* Glencoe, Ill.: Free Press, 1960.

Moynihan, Daniel. What is community action? *Public Interest,* Fall 1966, **5,** 3–8.

Nathan, Richard. Statement on revenue sharing. Senate Subcommittee on Intergovernmental Relations, June 5, 1974.

Nathan, Richard P., Manuel, Allen D., & Calkins, Susannah E. *Monitoring revenue sharing.* Washington, D.C.: The Brookings Institution, 1975.

National Opinion Research Corporation. *Fast deck codebook.* Chicago: University of Chicago, January 26, 1973.

Nie, Norman H., Hull, C. Hadlai, Jenkins, Jean G., Steinbrenner, Karin, & Bent, Dale H. *Statistical package for the social sciences.* (2nd ed.) New York: McGraw-Hill, 1975.

Oates, Wallace. Introduction, in Inman, Robert P., McGuire, Martin, Oates, Wallace E., Pressman, Jeffrey L., Reischauer, Robert D. *Financing the new federalism: revenue sharing, conditional grants, and taxation.* Baltimore: The Johns Hopkins University Press, 1975, pp. 13–39.

Office of Economic Opportunity. *A nation aroused: First annual report.* Washington, D.C., 1965.

Ohlin, Lloyd, & Cloward, Richard. *Delinquency and opportunity.* Glencoe, Ill.: Free Press, 1960.

Olds, Victoria. The freemen's bureau: A nineteenth-century federal welfare agency. *Social Casework,* May 1963, **44,** 251–252.

Peterson, Paul E., & Greenstone, J. David. Racial change and participation: The mobilization of low-income communities through community action," in Robert H. Haverman (Ed.) *A decade of federal antipoverty programs: achievements, failures, and lessons.* N.Y.: Academic Press, 1978.

Piven, Francis Fox, & Cloward, Richard A. *Regulating the poor: The functions of public welfare.* New York: Pantheon Books, 1971.

Powledge, Fred. *Model city.* New York: Simon and Schuster, 1970.

Pressman, Jeffrey L. Political Implications of the new federalism, in Inman, Robert P., McGuire, Martin, Oates, Wallace E., Pressman, Jeffrey L., Reischauer, Robert D. *Financing the new federalism: Revenue sharing, conditional grants, and taxation.* Baltimore: The Johns Hopkins University Press, 1975, pp. 13–39.

Presthus, Robert. *Men at the top: A study of community power.* New York: Oxford University Press, 1964.

Reagan, Michael D. *The new federalism.* New York: Oxford University Press, 1972.

Republican Coordinating Committee. *Financing the future of federalism: The case for revenue sharing.* Task Force on the Functions of Federal, State, and Local Government. Washington, D.C., March 1966.

Reston, James. *New York Times.* March 15, 1967.

Reuss, Henry S. *Revenue sharing: Crutch or catalyst for state and local governments?* New York: Praeger, 1970.

Rimlinger, Gaston. *Welfare policy and industrialization in Europe, America and Russia.* New York: John Wiley, 1971.

Rockefeller, Nelson A. *The future of federalism.* Cambridge, Mass.: Harvard University Press, 1968.

Rose, Stephen M. *The betrayal of the poor: The transformation of community action.* Cambridge, Mass.: Schenkman Publishing Company, 1972.

Rossi, Peter H., Berk, Richard A., & Eidson, Bettye K. *The roots of urban discontent.* New York: Wiley-Interscience, 1974.

Schneiderman, Leonard. Racism and Revenue Sharing. *Social Work,* May 1972, **17,** 44–49.

Sharkansky, Ira. Government expenditures and public services in the American states. *American Political Science Review,* December 1967, **61**, 1066–77.

State of Wisconsin, Department of Local Affairs and Development. "Memorandum." Madison, 1974.

Steiner, Gilbert. *The state of welfare.* Washington, D.C.: The Brookings Institute, 1971.

Steward Machine Company vs. **Davis,** 301 U.S. 548 (1937).

Subcommittee on Intergovernmental Relations, Committee on Governmental Operations, U.S. Senate. *Creative federalism.* 89th Congress, 2 Session, 1966, Part I.

Subcommittee on the Planning Process and Urban Development of the Department of Housing and Urban Development. *Revenue sharing and the planning process: Shifting the locus of responsibility for domestic problem solving.* Washington, D.C.: National Academy of Sciences, 1974.

Sundquist, James L., with the collaboration of David W. Davis. *Making federalism work: A study of program coordination at the community level.* Washington, D.C.: The Brookings Institution, 1969.

Sundquist, James L. *Politics and policy: The Eisenhower, Kennedy, and Johnson years.* Washington, D.C.: The Brookings Institution, 1968.

Titmus, Richard S. *Essays on the welfare state.* New Haven, Conn.: Yale University Press, 1959.

Trattner, Walter. *From poor law to welfare state: A history of social welfare in America.* New York: Free Press, 1974.

Trattner, Walter. The federal government and social welfare in early nineteenth-century America. *Social Service Review,* June 1976, **50**, 243–255.

Tufte, Edward R. *Data analysis for politics and policy.* Englewood Cliffs, N.J.: Prentice-Hall, 1974.

United States vs. **Butler,** 297 U.S. 1 (1936).

United States Constitution, Article IV, Section 3, Paragraph 2.

United States vs. **Darby,** 312 U.S. 100 (1941).

U.S. Department of Housing and Urban Development. "History of Congressional Action Relative to Model Cities, 1966–1967." Washington, D.C.: HUD, n.d.

U.S. Department of Housing and Urban Development. *HUD Statistical Yearbooks for 1970–71 and 1972.* Washington, D.C., 1972, 1974.

U.S. Department of Housing and Urban Development. "Model Cities Grants Approved Through 12/31/72" (mimeographed).

U.S. Department of Housing and Urban Development. "The Model Cities Program, Questions and Answers." Washington, D.C.: U.S. Government Printing Office, January 1970.

U.S. Department of the Treasury, Office of Revenue Sharing. *General Reve-*

nue Sharing: Reported Uses 1973–1974. Washington, D.C.: U.S. Printing Office, 1975.

U.S. Department of the Treasury, Office of Revenue Sharing. Xerox copies of General Revenue Sharing Actual Use Report for Each City for 1972–1974.

U.S. Office of Economic Opportunity. *Congressional Presentation.* Washington, D.C., April 1975.

U.S. Office of Economic Opportunity. *Directory of CAP Grantees.* Washington, D.C., February 1, 1966.

U.S. Office of Economic Opportunity. *Poverty Program Information as of January 1, 1966,* Washington, D.C., 1966.

Verba, Sidney, & Nie, Norman H. *Participation in America.* New York: Harper and Row, 1972.

Walton, John. "The bearing of social science research on public issues: Floyd Hunter and the study of power," in Walton, John, Carns, Donald E. *Cities in change: Studies on the urban social condition,* 2nd edition, Boston: Allyn and Bacon, Inc., 1977, pp. 263–72.

Warren, Roland. *The community in America,* 2nd edition, Chicago: Rand McNally and Co., 1972.

Wheeler, Gerald. Social welfare consequences of general revenue sharing. *Public Welfare,* Summer 1972, **30,** 3–10.

Wheeler, Gerald. New federalism and the cities: A double cross. *Social Work,* November 1974, **19,** 659–664.

Woodroofe, Kathleen. *From charity to social work in England and the United States.* Toronto: University of Toronto Press, 1962.

INDEX

United States Department of the
    Treasury, 39, 41, 113, 115,
    196
Secretary of Treasury, 39, 109
United States Supreme Court, 38,
    51, 55, 60–62, 65, 123–124
United States vs. *Butler* (1936),
    60
United States vs. *Darby* (1941),
    61
University of Chicago, 136, 149
Upward Bound, 177
Urban renewal, 64, 93, 133, 182
Utah, 34

Verba, Sidney, 140–141
Verbrugge, Lois M., 141
Veterans, 45, 56, 103
Vietnam War, 87, 89
Virginia, 42–43
Vocational Rehabilitation Act of
    1920, 56
Volunteers in Service to America,
    84, 86, 158

Walton, John, 132, 134
War on Poverty (*see* Poverty
    Program)
Warren, Roland, 138–139
Washington, D.C., 52, 75, 77, 86,
    95, 106, 110, 123
Weaver, Robert, 91
Weeks Act of 1911, 40–41
Welfare Clause of Constitution (*see*
    United States Constitution,
    general welfare clause)
Wheeler, Gerald, 105
Wirtz, Willard, 81
Wisconsin, 107
Woodroofe, Kathleen, 43
Worcester, Massachusetts, 116
Work Experience and Training
    Program, 83, 86, 158
Workmen's Compensation, 57
Works Progress Administration, 58
Work Study Program, 83, 85
World War I, 31, 52, 124
World War II, 32, 52, 124

Youth, 81, 113